CGP raises the curtain on GCSE Drama!

When it comes to GCSE Drama revision, there's a lot going on behind the scenes. But don't worry — this brilliant CGP book will give you a backstage pass...

It explains all the theory you need, from characterisation to design conventions, and there's plenty of top advice on the performance components too. Better yet, it's all illustrated with full-colour photos from real stage productions.

We've also squeezed in plenty of practice questions to test what you've learned, plus sample answers to show you how to pick up maximum marks. After all that, there'll be no chance of missing your cue in the exams!

CGP — still the best! ☺

Our sole aim here at CGP is to produce the highest quality books — carefully written, immaculately presented and dangerously close to being funny.

Then we work our socks off to get them out to you — at the cheapest possible prices.

Contents

Contents

Section Four — Devising

Section Five — Performance from a Text

Section Six — The Written Exam

Published by CGP

Editors:
Heather Cowley
Josh James
Kathryn Kaiser
Holly Robinson
James Summersgill
Jack Tooth

Contributors:
Carolyn Booth
Catherine Davis
Mike Vogler

With thanks to Matt Topping and Graham Fletcher for the proofreading.
With thanks to Emily Smith for the copyright research.

Acknowledgements:

With thanks to Photostage for permission to use the images on pages 4, 5, 8, 10, 14, 15, 17, 24, 29, 30, 33, 34, 35, 39, 40 & 46.

With thanks to ArenaPAL for permission to use the images on pages 1, 3, 6, 11, 16, 20, 21, 22, 25, 26, 27, 28, 36, 42, 45, 49, 51, 58 & 63.

With thanks to Alamy for permission to use the images on pages 9, 12, 13, 18 & 23.

With thanks to Mary Evans for permission to use the image on page 44.

ISBN: 978 1 78294 962 6
Printed by Elanders Ltd, Newcastle upon Tyne.
Clipart from Corel®

Based on the classic CGP style created by Richard Parsons.

Introduction to GCSE Drama

So you've chosen to do GCSE Drama — it might seem like a daunting prospect at this stage, but you've come to the right place. Here's what to expect as you work your way through this handy little guide to the course...

This book covers all of the theory...

© Johan Persson / ArenaPAL

1) GCSE Drama is a practical course, but it's underpinned by lots of theory — you'll need to learn it all before you think about treading the boards.
2) This book breaks down the theoretical side to drama into three sections:

- Section One covers the **THEATRE CONVENTIONS** that influence the way plays are performed, such as genre, structure and staging.
- Section Two focuses on **CHARACTERISATION AND PERFORMANCE**. It covers the performance skills that an actor uses to portray a character.
- Section Three is all about **DESIGN CONVENTIONS**. It's jam-packed with techniques that might be used to enhance the look and feel of a play.

... and shows you how to put it into practice

1) Once you've got to grips with the theory, you'll need to put it into practice in three assessed components:

Devised Performance

This component requires you to produce an original piece of theatre in response to a stimulus and keep a detailed record of the whole process (see Section Four).

Performance from a Text

You're also expected to stage a production of two extracts from a performance text. This can be done as an individual, as a pair or in a group (see Section Five).

Written Exam

The written exam is divided into two sections — it'll ask questions on a set text and a live performance that you have seen (see Section Six).

2) To earn marks in these assessed components, you'll have to meet different assessment objectives (AOs). These are the same across all exam boards:

These assessment objectives are weighted differently between each component — check this with your teacher.

Create and develop ideas to communicate meaning for theatrical performance (**AO1**).

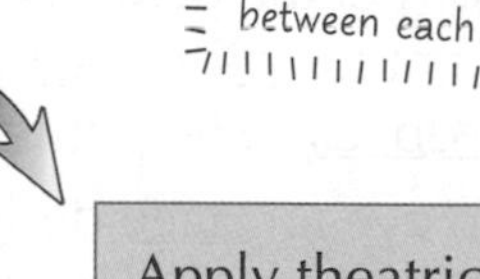

Apply theatrical skills to realise artistic intentions in live performance (**AO2**).

Demonstrate knowledge and understanding of how drama is developed and performed (**AO3**).

Analyse and evaluate your own work and the work of others (**AO4**).

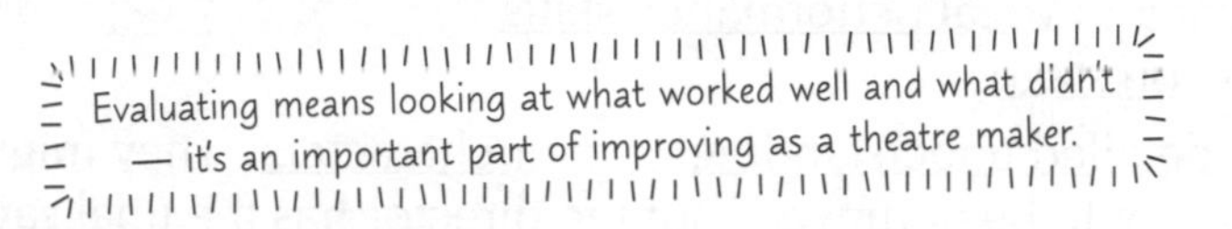

AO, AO, it's off to work we go...

You don't need to memorise these assessment objectives — they're just something to bear in mind when you start revising. Besides, you need to save room in that noggin of yours for the contents of this book...

Roles of Theatre Makers

Putting on a performance is no easy task — it takes a team of theatre makers with different expertise. These are most of the positions that need filling before your thoughts can turn to the opening night.

Theatre makers work together to make their show a success

1) 'Theatre maker' is the term given to anyone who is involved in staging a performance. Playwrights, directors, performers and costume designers are just some examples of theatre makers.
2) Large-scale productions (for example a play in the West End) will employ hundreds of theatre makers, whereas smaller-scale performances (for example a one-woman play in a village hall) might only need a couple. Sometimes, one person might take on several different roles within a production, e.g. the same person could write, direct and perform a play.
3) Although theatre makers have different roles and responsibilities, they have to work together to make sure their performance is successful. For this to happen, it needs to be popular with audiences, so it's really important that theatre makers think about the effect on the audience at all times.

Playwrights write the script

1) Almost every performance needs a script — this is written by a playwright. Some playwrights write scripts with lots of details on how it could be performed (this is shown through stage directions — see p.10). Others include very little detail and leave performance decisions up to the director or performer.
2) Sometimes a script isn't fixed — it might evolve during rehearsals.
3) If the performance has songs, then a composer and lyricist will write them to accompany the script.

The director decides how the play is performed

1) The director has creative control over how a playwright's work is brought to the stage.
2) After choosing a performance text, the director needs to develop a clear vision of how they want it to be performed. It's their responsibility to pass on this vision to everyone involved in the production so they can carry out their own roles effectively.
3) It's also the director's job to audition performers and oversee the rehearsals, where they instruct the performers on everything from positioning and movement to delivering their lines. They also give performers feedback to help them improve.
4) The director needs to have an eye for stage design too. A team of designers might come up with lots of different ideas, but the director needs to bring these ideas together in a consistent way.

Types of Rehearsal

The director needs to oversee a few different types of rehearsal in the lead-up to a performance. The technical rehearsal focuses on aspects of design such as the lighting and sound, whereas the dress rehearsal is a run-through of the whole play during which all performers are in costume.

The performers bring the director's vision to life

1) The performers (or actors) use a range of physical and vocal performance skills (see Section Two) to achieve the director's vision on stage.
2) Their main task is to learn the script and gain a detailed understanding of their characters. They might have some suggestions for how their characters should be portrayed, but the director has the final say.
3) The performers need to work as a team — not just with the other performers, but also with the designers whose job it is to add emphasis to their performance. In some productions, the performers might also have to work with understudies.

An understudy is someone who learns a performer's role so that they can replace them if necessary.

Roles of Theatre Makers

The designers specialise in particular areas

1) Much like the performers, the designers (see Section Three) have an important role in making sure that the director's vision is achieved. Their roles are often so technical that they have to specialise:

- A **LIGHTING DESIGNER** decides which lighting to use. They draw up a lighting plot — a list of all the lighting changes that take place in the production.
- A **SOUND DESIGNER** creates a sound plot which outlines what sound effects and music are required. They may also arrange microphones for the performers.
- A **SET DESIGNER** designs the scenery, furniture and props. They provide sketches of their designs and suggest materials, before overseeing the construction process.
- A **COSTUME DESIGNER** is responsible for clothing, hair and make-up. Their ideas need to contribute to the production by fitting in with the context of the play.
- A **PUPPET DESIGNER** creates puppets if the production needs them. As well as matching the style of the production, these puppets need to be easy to operate.
- A **CHOREOGRAPHER** designs any dance routines. They may help teach and rehearse the routines with the performers or work closely with the composer.

2) As well as communicating with the director, the designers have to talk to the performers to check if their designs are causing any difficulties. For example, a costume that matches the director's vision perfectly might restrict the movement of the performer who has to wear it during the performance.
3) All designers need to be problem solvers. It's normal for technical problems to occur at some point, but it's a designer's responsibility to offer creative solutions that don't cost too much time or money.

Every theatre production has its unsung heroes

1) Some roles are less glamorous than others, but they're just as important. These roles include the theatre manager, who is responsible for a theatre's front-of-house staff (e.g. the box office staff and ushers).
2) The stage manager runs everything that happens backstage. They organise the rehearsal schedule and create a prompt book with the help of their deputy stage manager.

The prompt book is an annotated copy of the script that contains every detail about the performance, including technical cues.

3) A team of technicians operate the technical equipment during a performance — it's the stage manager's role to supervise them.
4) The stage manager also gives cues to other theatre makers — they ensure that the lighting, sound and scenery changes at the right time, and that the performers are on stage when they're supposed to be.
5) Stagehands work backstage — they set up and change scenery and props.

REVISION TASK

The butcher, the baker, the theatre maker...

Create a spider diagram containing all the different theatre makers involved in putting on a performance. Make sure you consider all of the following points:

1) The roles and responsibilities of theatre makers.
2) The relationships between different theatre makers.
3) The potential challenges faced by theatre makers.

Tick list:
✓ accurate terminology
✓ roles of theatre makers before / during a play

Theatre in Context

Unless you get to grips with its context, a play isn't going to make a lot of sense.

Context is crucial to understanding a play...

1) Context is the background to a play, including when and where the play was either written or set.
2) Context can be divided into three categories — historical, social and cultural (although these can overlap):

Historical Context

Historical context refers to any major events that happened at the time the play was written or set, for example religious conflict or political upheaval.

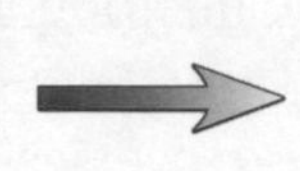

The Crucible is set during the Salem witch trials — a series of court cases that ended in several executions. The plot revolves around the trials, as well as the fear and uncertainty they caused.

Social Context

Social context is the way most people thought, behaved and lived at a given time, which includes things like class, gender roles and attitudes towards race.

An Inspector Calls is set in 1912, but was written in 1945. Priestley uses the huge divide between working-class and wealthy characters in the play to highlight the continuing inequality in 1945.

Cultural Context

Cultural context refers to any trends or interests that were popular at the time, such as music, film and television.

Blood Brothers contains multiple references to Marilyn Monroe, a famous actress who died in 1962 — around the same time as the play is set.

3) A playwright is often commenting on a particular element of the play's context through their writing — they might use the play to deliver a social, political or moral message to the audience.

... and it has an impact on how the play is performed

1) When writing about a play's context, it's important to link it closely to how the play looks on stage.
2) Context has an impact on aspects of design like scenery and costume. If these aren't done properly, it's much harder to give the audience an accurate impression of when and where the play is set.
3) However, the importance of context goes beyond telling the audience about the setting — it can also be used to reveal more about characters' personalities, relationships and backgrounds.
4) Actors can use physical and vocal skills to give the audience more information about context:

A 2007 production of 'Blood Brothers' using 1960s clothes.

- Physical performance (see p.24-27) includes things like movement, posture and eye contact. Negative attitudes towards characters of a particular gender, race or class are part of the social context. This can be shown by an actor's lack of eye contact or closed body language.
- Vocal performance (see p.28-30) includes things like tone of voice, volume and accent. Actors can use different accents to give the audience an idea of their characters' backgrounds.

Theatre in Context

Directors don't have to stick to the original context

1) Some directors choose to set their plays in a different context to the original to highlight a certain message. This is common in modern interpretations of plays written by Shakespeare (1564-1616).
2) Shakespeare's plays were written a long time ago, but they deal with themes like war, revenge, love and family relationships. These themes are universal — they're just as relevant to audiences now as they were during the 1600s.

Macbeth

- *Macbeth*'s key themes of power and ambition make it well-suited to a modern setting. A 2007 production at the Chichester Festival Theatre took the play (set in medieval Scotland) and set it in Soviet Russia.
- To reflect this context, the actors wore clothes that were typical of Russia in the mid-1900s and used modern props like guns. Most of the action took place in an underground bunker.
- By changing the context, the director could approach the play's main themes differently. For example, Macbeth's brutal rise to power is linked to Stalin — a Russian dictator who was known for his cruelty.

© Donald Cooper / photostage

The purpose of theatre has changed over time

It's important to think about the purpose of theatre when a play was written. People's reasons for going to the theatre have changed, which means that different types of drama have been popular at different times. It's also useful to consider how audiences' reactions have changed. For example, a play that would have been shocking to Victorian audiences may not have the same impact on a 21st-century audience.

1) In medieval times, theatre was dominated by the Church, so performances aimed to educate audiences about Christianity as well as being entertaining. Plays would usually be stories from the Bible.
2) In the 16th and 17th centuries, a style of theatre known as *commedia dell'arte* developed in Italy and became popular across Western Europe. Companies of professional actors travelled between towns and cities to entertain the masses with their humorous (and often improvised) performances.
3) During the Restoration, people in England embraced the theatre as a form of entertainment again after a long time of not being able to go at all. These plays often mocked 17th-century society, but did it in a light-hearted way with lots of witty dialogue.
4) In the 20th century, European theatre generally became more serious. After the extreme violence of the Second World War, going to the theatre was seen as an opportunity for people to make sense of life.

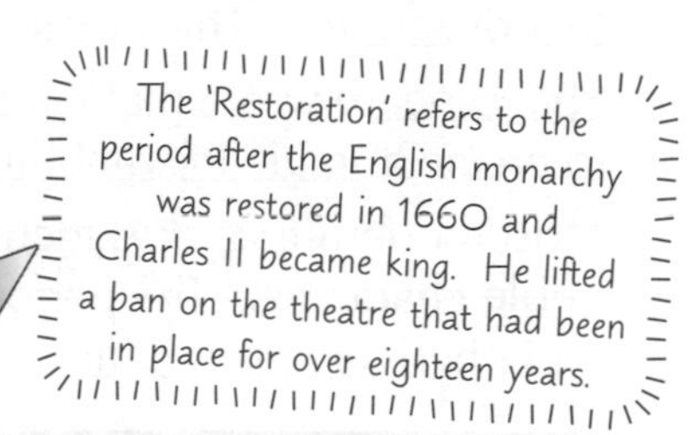

Fair is foul, and foul is... wait, is that a gun?

Write a paragraph about the context of a play you've studied. Make sure you answer all of the following questions:

1) When was the play written?
2) When and where is the play set?
3) How might context affect the director's decisions about a play? Give five examples of decisions a director might make.

Tick list:
✓ impact of context
✓ different interpretations
✓ director's methods

Form and Genre

FORM is the type of drama — this is decided by the **PLAYWRIGHT**.

Different forms have their own theatrical conventions

Performances can be categorised into different forms. Each form has its own set of conventions — things that the audience would expect from the performance. Here are some examples:

FORM	CONVENTIONS
PLAY	Dialogue (either scripted or improvised) between several characters.
MUSICAL	Some dialogue between characters, but also some singing and dancing.
MIME	The performer(s) should remain silent and convey meaning through movement and facial expressions.
MONOLOGUE	One performer who talks directly to the audience.

© Marilyn Kingwill / ArenaPAL

'Singin' in the Rain' is an example of a musical.

The **GENRE** refers to what type of story a performance tells — this is up to the **PLAYWRIGHT**.

Tragedies are serious...

1) Tragedy is a genre that was originally developed by the Ancient Greeks.
2) Tragedies typically have a serious plot and a sad ending — often the death of one or more main characters. Rather than trying to create humour, tragedies aim to produce 'catharsis'.

Greek Tragedy

This is a type of play in the tragedy genre. A Greek tragedy is about a flawed character (the 'tragic hero') who eventually meets their downfall. This character tends to be a powerful figure, like a king, whose fate seems more important as a result.

3) Catharsis is when the tragic events of a play make the audience feel strong emotions of their own, like fear or sadness. This creates an emotional release, allowing the audience to get rid of these emotions.
4) Shakespeare wrote many tragedies (e.g. *Macbeth*). He used techniques such as foreshadowing to create a tragic inevitability — the feeling that the fate of the hero is unavoidable.
5) Most modern tragedies focus on characters from more normal backgrounds, rather than high-status or noble characters. The performers can encourage the audience to relate to their characters using vocal and physical performance — this can make these plays even more likely to produce catharsis.

© Fritz Curzon / ArenaPAL

A 1996 performance of 'Death of a Salesman'.

Death of a Salesman

Death of a Salesman is a tragedy by Arthur Miller. The tragic hero is Willy Loman — an ageing salesman from New York City who becomes gradually more unstable as the play goes on. He isn't as high-status as a traditional tragic hero, but his death still seems tragic because he's so relatable. The performer playing Willy Loman often uses a working-class accent to add to the sense that he's a normal person.

6) A tragicomedy is a play that contains elements of both tragedy and comedy and can't be easily classified as either. Shakespeare wrote several plays that are now classed as tragicomedies, such as *Measure for Measure*. This play has a happy ending, but it also contains lots of sad moments and tackles serious themes like justice, mercy and death.

Form and Genre

... whereas comedies are more light-hearted

1) Comedy as a genre dates all the way back to Ancient Greece. Comedies typically feature a light-hearted plot, witty dialogue and a happy ending for the main characters.
2) Shakespeare was responsible for developing this genre in the 16th and 17th centuries. He created humour using techniques like wordplay, mistaken identity and dramatic irony (see p.11).
3) Many plays in this genre rely on visual comedy to entertain the audience — the characters' appearances and actions can create as much humour as their words. Sometimes, props can be a source of humour, particularly in a slapstick comedy.

Slapstick is a type of physical comedy that often uses clumsy actions like actors falling over or props being broken.

4) Comedy can be divided into sub-genres, for example:

- A farce uses improbable situations and physical humour to entertain the audience.
- A parody makes fun of an existing piece of work (e.g. another play) by imitating it.
- A satire mocks something serious (e.g. politics) by highlighting how ridiculous it is.

Melodramas have lots of plot twists

1) A melodrama is a genre of play characterised by unbelievable plots, extreme emotions and exaggerated acting. Most plays in this genre are stories about love with a happy ending.
2) The characters in melodramas are often stock characters (a kind of character stereotype — see p.21), so the play focuses more on the plot than on character development or growth.
3) Music features heavily in melodramas, but doesn't contribute to the plot — incidental music plays in the background to add to the overall mood. For example, music can give the audience a better idea of the intense emotions that the characters are feeling at a particular moment (see p.36-37 for more on music).

Documentary theatre is based on true events

1) Documentary theatre is a more recent genre that takes stories from real life and brings them to the stage.
2) The plot, characters and script are taken from factual sources like newspapers, letters and interviews. For example, *Black Watch* (2006) was based on interviews with soldiers who served in the Black Watch regiment during the Iraq War. Using these sources allows documentary theatre makers to portray real-life events in an authentic way.
3) In some cases, the performers repeat the source material word for word — this is called verbatim theatre, and it's a popular way for modern theatre companies to deliver strong messages about topical issues.

Recorded Delivery

Recorded Delivery is a verbatim theatre company that uses interviews with real people as a starting point for the script. These interviews are edited into a structure that works for the stage, but the exact wording is left unchanged. The actors listen to this recording through earphones while they're performing and reproduce every detail, including coughs and hesitations. Recorded Delivery tackle current issues such as social conflict. For example, *Little Revolution* is about the London riots in 2011. Their approach presents the audience with a range of different perspectives and makes it easier for them to form an opinion.

Not to make a song and dance about form and genre, but...

... it's really important that you get to grips with the different forms and genres and their characteristics. If you do, you'll find it much easier to write about the plays you study in class and watch at the theatre.

Dramatic Structure

All plays need structure — without it, they'd just be a sticky mess in the middle of the stage. Luckily for you, everything you need to know is right here on these pages. All that's left for you to do is read them carefully.

Certain structures are traditional...

1) Plays are traditionally divided into acts and scenes. An act is a larger section of a play that can contain several scenes, while a scene is defined as a shorter section that takes place at one time or in one place.
2) The main use of act and scene changes is to switch between different times and locations, which can be shown using the set. However, scene changes can also signal a shift in mood using lighting and sound.
3) Until the 18th century, five-act plays were most common. Most follow the same dramatic structure:

Some performances might start with a prologue. This is a short introduction to the story which gives the audience some background details.

Act One — The **EXPOSITION** in Act One introduces the main characters and hints at a conflict they'll face later.

Act Two — The **RISING ACTION** in Act Two develops the conflict introduced during the exposition to build tension.

Act Three — The **CLIMAX** in Act Three is the turning point, where the drama and tension are at their highest. An **ANTICLIMAX** might take place if the tension is suddenly relieved.

Act Four — The **FALLING ACTION** in Act Four settles the conflict, but there may be one last moment of suspense.

Act Five — The **RESOLUTION** in Act Five ties up any loose ends that are left over from the falling action.

Some performances might end with an epilogue. Epilogues can be used to summarise or comment on the ending.

4) Another conventional structure is the three-act play. Most three-act plays have a similar dramatic structure to five-act plays — Act One introduces all of the main characters, Act Two develops these characters and builds up to the climax, and Act Three relieves the tension and brings the action to a close.

... but they're far from the only options

1) The structure of modern plays is more flexible than it used to be — most plays written since the 19th century contain fewer than five acts, and these aren't always separated into scenes.
2) In modern theatre, two-act plays are particularly common. This is partly for practical reasons — dividing a play into two parts allows for the audience to have an interval in the middle. However, a two-act structure can also affect the pace of the play and create different types of atmosphere.
3) Other plays consist of a series of short scenes (or episodes) that are linked only by a character, a location or a theme. Episodic structure can provide a broad overview of a subject — in *Dr Korczak's Example*, it allows the audience to see different aspects of the treatment of Polish Jews during World War Two.
4) Some plays aren't divided into acts and scenes at all. These one-act plays usually have fewer characters and locations, but they can be used by a playwright to focus on one issue in detail without distracting the audience.

Blood Brothers

Blood Brothers contains two acts, but no scenes — the action flows continuously from one part of the story to another. This means that it's a particularly fast-paced play.

A 1996 production of 'Endgame', a one-act play by Samuel Beckett.

Dramatic Structure

The plot is the main story being told

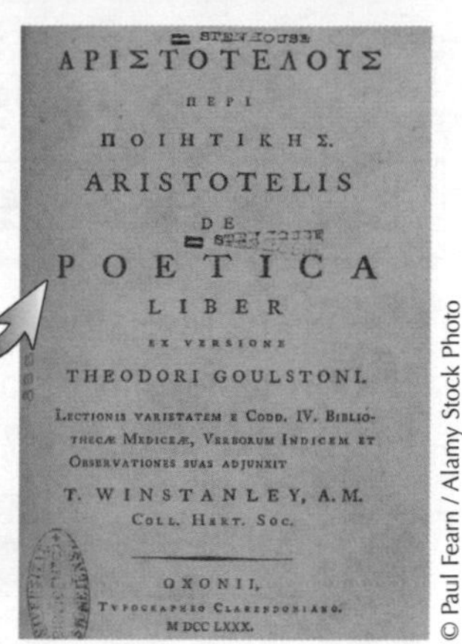

© Paul Fearn / Alamy Stock Photo

1) The plot (or the narrative) is the series of events that takes place during a play. As a general rule, all plays need a plot with a beginning, a middle and an end.
2) According to the Ancient Greeks, all plays should have one main plot to avoid unnecessary distractions. In a famous guide to dramatic theory called *Poetics*, Aristotle (384-322 BC) wrote that the plot is the most important element of a play, because this is what brings out an emotional reaction from the audience.
3) Conflict is a key feature of any plot, but this doesn't always take the form of a disagreement between characters. In some plays, the conflict is a problem that needs solving or an obstacle that one of the characters has to overcome.
4) How this conflict is resolved depends mainly on the genre of the play (see p.6-7). Comedies have happy endings, but tragedies end in a way that causes pain, suffering or even death for the characters involved.

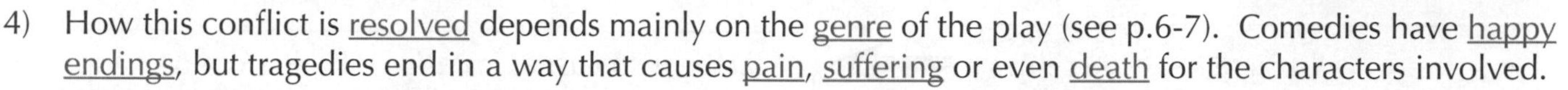

5) Not all plays have a decisive ending — some end on a cliffhanger. If a particular aspect of the conflict isn't fully resolved, it builds tension and unsettles the audience by making them guess what will happen.

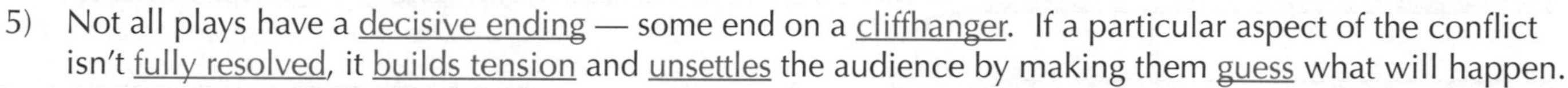

Subplots are minor storylines

1) Subplots add complexity to a story without drawing the audience's attention away from the main plot.
2) Most subplots contribute to the main plot in some way. They might reveal more about the characters, or look at a key theme from a new perspective.
3) Subplots can also make a play more varied — they might focus on different characters and explore different issues from the main plot. They might also have a different tone from the main plot of the play.

Twelfth Night

The main plot of *Twelfth Night* is about Viola, who has been shipwrecked and disguises herself as a man. She becomes involved in a love triangle with Orsino and Olivia. This plot is woven together with subplots:

- Viola's brother also survives the shipwreck and makes his way to Orsino's house.
- Olivia's steward, Malvolio, is tricked into believing that Olivia is in love with him.

Plots and subplots can be linear or non-linear

1) If a plot advances chronologically (in the same order as the events happened), it's called a linear plot. It's easier for the audience to immerse themselves in a linear plot, because it's more realistic (see p.12).
2) However, not all plots progress chronologically — some jump backwards and forwards between different times and locations. These are known as non-linear plots, and they're a useful way of creating effects like dramatic irony (see p.11).
3) Some plots give the audience a sense that events are inevitable by starting and finishing the story in the same place — these are called cyclical plots. Cyclical plots can create suspense and tension because the audience knows how the play will end so they can anticipate what is going to happen.

Time and the Conways

Time and the Conways has a non-linear plot — it starts in 1919, flashes forward to 1937, then picks up where it left off in 1919 again.

Blood Brothers

Blood Brothers has a cyclical plot — it starts and ends with the deaths of Mickey and Edward.

Use these pages to plot your way to exam success...

No matter what genre a play belongs to, structure and plot are going to form its basic foundations. That means you need to be confident writing about them before you move on to the smaller details.

Conventions of Theatre

No two plays are the same, but most of them share lots of the same features — the conventions of theatre. Sounds interesting, right...? Well try to contain your excitement, because it's really important to learn them.

Some stage directions are more detailed than others

1) Stage directions are instructions written in a script to explain how a play should be performed.
2) In older plays, stage directions are mainly used to tell the performers when to enter and exit the stage. In contrast, many modern playwrights write extremely detailed stage directions to describe things like:

- the characters' movements  MR PECK *turns round and sees* MRS WELSH. *He freezes.*

  Blue Stockings — Jessica Swale

- the way characters say their lines  WILLY: (*with casual irritation)* I said nothing happened.

  Death of a Salesman — Arthur Miller

- the scenery, props and furniture  *It has good solid furniture of the period.*

  An Inspector Calls — J.B. Priestley

3) However, this doesn't apply to all modern plays — some (e.g. *DNA*) have hardly any stage directions. This gives the director the freedom to adapt these plays to suit their own ideas.
4) Directors don't have to follow the stage directions at all. For example, if the director wants to change the setting of a play (see p.5), they might decide to ignore certain stage directions entirely.

There are specific terms for what the characters say...

1) Scripts are normally split up into lines, with character names at the side to show who says what.
2) The general term for lines spoken between characters is dialogue, but there are other types of speech:

- A **DUOLOGUE** is when two characters have a conversation together.
- A **MONOLOGUE** is when a character makes a speech to another character or the audience.
- A **SOLILOQUY** is when a character talks to themselves to express their feelings. This gets the audience emotionally involved in the character, because they can tell they're being honest.
- An **ASIDE** is when a character make a comment to another character or the audience, but the rest of the characters on stage can't hear them. This can be done for comic effect.

... and narrators to fill in what they don't

'omniscient' means 'all-knowing'.

1) Some plays use narrators to give the audience extra information. It's also a common way of breaking the fourth wall (see p.12).
2) If someone comments on the action without taking part, they're a third-person narrator. Many third-person narrators are omniscient, so they're able to tell the audience what the characters are thinking. Greek tragedies (see p.6) often used multiple third-person narrators to provide extra information — these were known as the 'chorus'.
3) If a character who's involved in the action shares their own point of view on what's happening, they become a first-person narrator.
4) It's important to think about where the narrator is placed on stage. Placing a narrator downstage (see p.18) makes them seem important.

'Blood Brothers' by Willy Russell contains a third-person narrator.

Conventions of Theatre

Dramatic irony can create humour and tension

Dramatic irony is when the audience knows something the characters don't. It's created in different ways...

- The audience might witness an important event that some of the characters aren't on stage to see.
- A character could reveal hidden thoughts and feelings to the audience in a soliloquy or an aside.
- Disguises allow the characters to hide their true identity, but the audience can see through them.

... and it can have different effects:

- Dramatic irony can create humour. The audience can see that Bottom has a donkey's head in *A Midsummer Night's Dream*, but he can't tell. It's funny to watch the confusion this causes.
- It can also be used to create tension. The audience knows Juliet is just sleeping at the end of *Romeo and Juliet*, but Romeo thinks she's dead. They can only look on as Romeo kills himself.

Marking the moment grabs the audience's attention

1) Some moments are so significant that they need highlighting — this is called marking the moment.
2) Ways of marking the moment include a tableau. This is when all of the performers freeze at a certain moment to cement it in the minds of the audience.
3) A freeze frame is another way of marking the moment — this is when a character 'steps out' of a scene and reveals something to the audience while the rest of the action freezes.
4) The use of slow motion also marks the moment — it makes the audience pay close attention to the performers' actions.

'The Government Inspector' famously ends with a tableau.

Flashbacks and flashforwards play around with time

1) Flashbacks are scenes which go back in time. They're a way of creating a non-linear plot (see p.9) without causing the audience too much confusion.
2) Plays can also flash forward to show the audience events that will happen in the future. This provides the audience with clues about what is going to happen later in the story and can create dramatic irony.
3) Flashbacks and flashforwards are used to reveal information that the audience didn't know before, or to show a new side to a character. As a result, their effect on the audience is usually shock or surprise.
4) Both flashbacks and flashforwards can be included in the same scene using cross-cutting. This is when two or more scenes that take place in different times or places are performed on stage at the same time.

This book's got more drama than a theatre convention...

Create a spider diagram containing the conventions of theatre that appear in a play of your choice. Make sure you answer the following questions:

1) What is the play's genre and structure?
2) What information is there in the stage directions?
3) What other theatre conventions does the playwright use?

Tick list:
✓ appropriate vocabulary
✓ effect on the audience
✓ examples from the play

Style

The **STYLE** of a play refers to **HOW** it's performed on stage — this is up to the **DIRECTOR**.

Some theatre makers try to replicate real life...

1) Naturalism is a style of theatre that aims to recreate real life as closely as possible on stage.
2) Every aspect of the performance has to be believable, including the scenery, lighting and sound. Theatre makers may choose a naturalistic style because they want to make the audience suspend their disbelief and be fully entertained by the action on stage.
3) To maintain the illusion of real life, the performers can't break the fourth wall by addressing the audience directly or acknowledging that they're taking part in a play — they have to stay in character.
4) One important practitioner of naturalism was Konstantin Stanislavski:

A theatre style that's particularly realistic is sometimes described as 'realism'.

The Fourth Wall

The 'fourth wall' is the name given to the imagined barrier that separates the performers on stage from the audience.

Konstantin Stanislavski — Naturalism

- Konstantin Stanislavski (1863-1938) was a Russian actor and director. He thought that creating believable characters was the key to convincing the audience that what they were watching was real.
- He encouraged actors to develop a detailed backstory for their characters and use this to understand what motivated their actions. Part of this is the 'magic if' technique, where actors imagine how their characters would react if they faced different questions or were in different fictional situations.
- He thought that an actor's performance would be more believable if they used emotional memory and drew on their own experiences, e.g. drawing on a painful memory to portray a sad character.
- He believed a sense of isolation on stage could help actors to relax and develop their characterisation. His circles of attention encourage actors to focus primarily on themselves (the first circle), then on other characters they're talking to (the second) and finally on the rest of the production (the third).

... but others do their best to avoid it

1) One criticism of naturalism is that it makes the audience lose themselves in the story instead of urging them to think critically about what they're watching. This makes it difficult to explore serious issues.
2) Non-naturalistic theatre is the opposite of naturalism — it aims to distance the audience from the story by reminding them that it isn't real. This encourages the audience to focus on the play's message.
3) One type of non-naturalistic theatre is epic theatre, which is associated with Bertolt Brecht:

Minimalist or abstract theatre styles are non-naturalistic (see p.32 for more).

Bertolt Brecht — Epic Theatre

- Bertolt Brecht (1898-1956) was a German playwright and director.
- Epic theatre uses techniques to remind the audience that they are watching a play — this is known as the 'alienation effect'.
- These techniques include breaking the fourth wall, the use of narration (see p.10) and a non-linear structure that jumps between different times and places. This style of theatre often uses minimal scenery and props and contains characters that aren't fully developed.
- The aim of these techniques is to allow the audience to focus on the (usually political) message of the play.
- Brecht's plays would often contrast comedy with serious issues — they 'tickle' the audience with something funny and then 'slap' them with something serious.

Style

Theatre of Cruelty uses shock tactics

1) Theatre of Cruelty is a style developed by French actor and director Antonin Artaud (1896-1948).
2) Like Brecht, Artaud believed that theatre should make the audience think, but he took this idea further — he wanted to shock the audience into feeling extreme emotions and use his plays to release them.

© Paul Fearn / Alamy Stock Photo

3) Artaud thought that productions should assault the audience's senses with a combination of bright lights, loud sound effects and striking movements and gestures. He thought these techniques lent themselves to communicating strong emotions to the audience and were more effective than dialogue.
4) Artaud also wanted to change the relationship between the audience and the performers. He suggested sitting the audience in the middle of an empty room with the performance going on around them to make watching it an even more intense and powerful experience.
5) Artaud only ever applied his ideas to one play — *Les Cenci* (1935). It was a total failure, but Artaud's style inspired other theatre makers to start experimenting with similar techniques in their own work.
6) The failure of *Les Cenci* highlights the importance of the audience for a production. If a play is so violent, unpleasant or shocking that an audience won't watch it, then a theatre maker can't achieve the aims of their play or successfully deliver their message.

Theatre of the Oppressed gets the audience to take action

1) Augusto Boal (1931-2009) didn't think it was enough for the audience to watch a play — he thought the only way to bring about a positive change in their attitudes was to make them take an active role.
2) He came up with Theatre of the Oppressed, which uses a range of techniques to get the audience involved.
3) One of the main techniques developed by Boal was invisible theatre. This involved putting on a performance in public, but disguising it as real life. The idea was that the 'audience' would choose to intervene in the performance without actually realising what was happening.

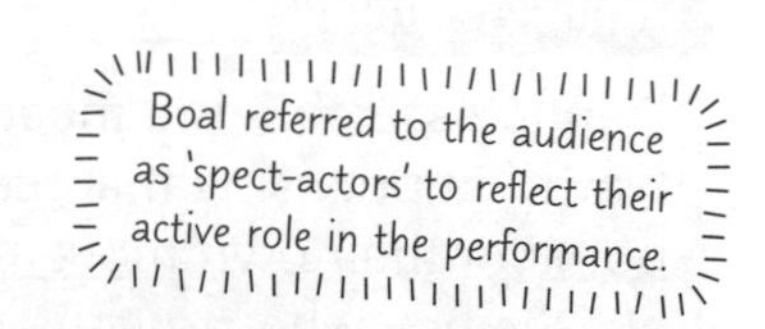

4) However, Boal's most well-known technique is called forum theatre:

- In forum theatre, a short play featuring a form of injustice (e.g. sexism) is performed twice. During the second performance, the audience is expected to change the play's outcome by participating.
- The audience's role varies — in some cases, they're asked to stop the performers and suggest what they should do differently. In others, they're actually invited to act out their suggestions themselves.
- The idea of getting the audience to participate in the performance is that after tackling injustice in a theatre, they'll realise that they're capable of making a difference in real-life situations too.
- Any interaction between the audience and the performers is managed by a 'joker'. The joker decides if and when the audience can intervene, as well as leading a discussion with the audience afterwards.

5) Several theatre companies use these ideas to try to bring about positive change. This style of theatre is particularly popular with many social and political movements as a way of raising awareness for the problems faced by modern society.

Cardboard Citizens

Cardboard Citizens is a theatre company whose actors have all been homeless in the past. They use forum theatre to make people think about the issue of homelessness and what can be done to solve it.

Style

As if that wasn't enough, here are a couple more styles for you to get your head around...

Immersive theatre brings the audience closer

1) Like Theatre of the Oppressed, immersive theatre removes the barrier between the performers and the audience. However, its purpose isn't always to get across a serious message — it's to be entertaining.
2) Immersive theatre takes different forms. It might involve the audience being led between multiple performance spaces, or they might be allowed to move freely, with the action going on around them. In some cases, they might even be asked to join in.
3) By changing the relationship between the actors and the audience, immersive theatre alters the audience's expectations of what a 'normal' theatre experience is like — it's exciting for them to feel part of the action.

Site-Specific Staging

Immersive theatre is suited to site-specific staging (p.17) — this staging offers interesting surroundings for the audience to explore.

Physical theatre uses movement to convey meaning

1) Physical theatre is a style which uses choreographed movement and dancing to tell a story on stage. These movements can be combined with traditional dialogue, or used all on their own.
2) To allow the audience to concentrate on the movement, physical theatre productions often use minimal props and scenery. In some cases, the actors' bodies are even used as objects on stage.
3) In this way, physical theatre builds on the ideas of Brecht and Artaud (see p.12-13) — there's nothing realistic about this sort of movement.
4) This style allows physical theatre companies to communicate emotions to the audience that would be difficult to get across using only words.

© Donald Cooper / photostage

Frantic Assembly

Frantic Assembly is a theatre company that uses a technique called contact improvisation — a way of improvising that requires the performers to use physical contact with others as the starting point for their own movements. *The Curious Incident of the Dog in the Night-Time* is about an autistic boy who struggles to express himself. Frantic Assembly used physical theatre to give the audience an insight into his thoughts. For example, unnatural movements and chaotic scenes featuring lots of performers highlighted the boy's struggle to understand the world around him.

Steven Berkoff

British theatre practitioner Berkoff (born 1937) is known for his experimental style. His plays often use physical theatre techniques like mime, exaggerated movements and improvisation — he believes that actors' bodies should convey the story rather than relying on sets.

A revision task — the best way to end a page in style...

Choose two plays that you've seen. Write a list of the similarities and differences in their style. Make sure you answer all of the following questions:

1) Are these plays trying to replicate real life or not?
2) What message (if any) are these plays trying to get across?
3) Do these plays require any involvement from the audience?

Tick list:
✓ technical terminology
✓ director's intentions
✓ director's methods

Staging

Once you've chosen a style, you're going to need a stage — and again, there's plenty to choose from...

Proscenium arch stages are set back from the audience

A proscenium arch stage is a box-shaped performance space that is set back from the audience — only the front end is open. The 'proscenium arch' is the frame that separates the audience from the stage. Some proscenium arch stages have an apron that extends into the audience.

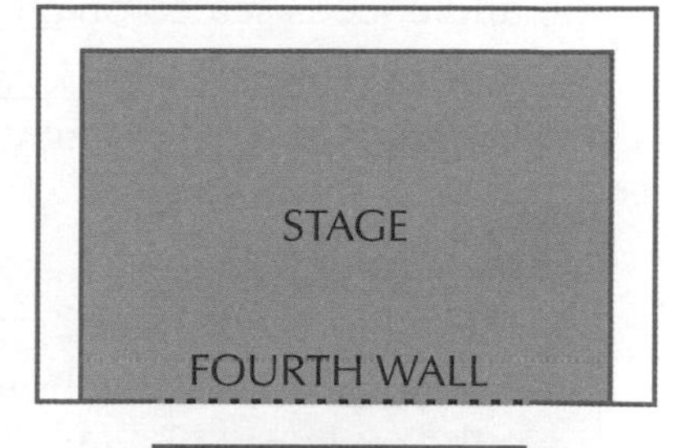

Pros

- They're ideal for naturalistic plays — the distance between the actors and audience helps to maintain the fourth wall (p.12).
- The audience is all facing the same way so it's possible to use detailed backdrops and bigger pieces of scenery without interrupting sightlines. Blocking is easier with this stage too.
- There's lots of space in the wings and backstage for storage.

Blocking is the process of working out where all the actors are standing to make sure everyone in the audience can see them (see p.26).

Cons

- The distance between actors and audience can cause problems. The audience may struggle to feel involved, particularly if they're sitting at the back of the theatre. In some cases, they might not be able to see or hear properly.
- The proscenium arch makes things feel more 'formal' so it could be less suited to non-naturalistic or physical theatre.

A proscenium arch.

End-on staging is similar to a proscenium arch stage, but without the arch to frame the stage. The lack of the proscenium arch can make the theatre feel less 'grand', which might suit non-naturalistic productions.

Thrust stages stick out into the audience

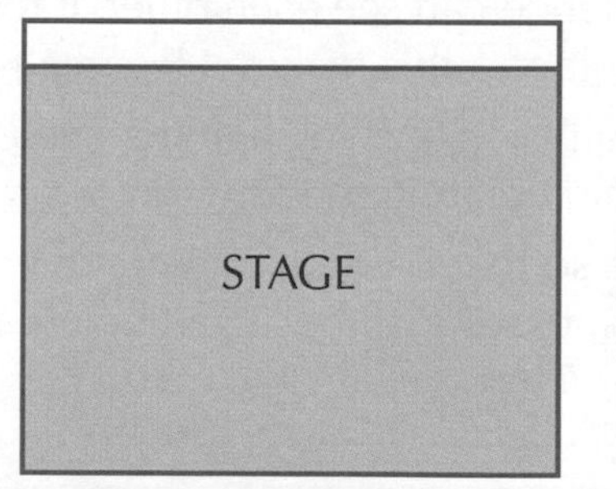

The front of a thrust stage (or apron) extends into the audience so that they're seated on three sides of it. Some thrust stages have a proscenium arch, but performers can move beyond it without breaking the fourth wall (unlike on a proscenium arch stage).

Pros

- A thrust stage closes the gap between the performers and the audience. Having the audience on three sides of the stage helps to create an intimate atmosphere.
- There's still a back wall to the stage which means backdrops and large pieces of scenery can be used.

Cons

- It limits the type of sets that can be used e.g. box sets (see p.70) can't be used. Unless scenery is placed against the back wall, it could obstruct the audience's view.
- Blocking is trickier — it's hard to maintain sightlines for the audience on three sides at the same time.

A thrust stage, viewed from the back of the stage.

Staging

These stage configurations may not be as common as the ones on p.15, but they're still well worth learning.

The audience surrounds the stage in theatre in the round

1) The audience is seated on all sides of the stage in theatre in the round.
2) The lack of wings or a backstage area means the performers have to enter and exit using walkways through the audience.

AUDIENCE | AUDIENCE | STAGE | AUDIENCE | AUDIENCE

Pros

- Theatre in the round creates an even more intimate atmosphere than a thrust stage — it's good for making the audience feel fully immersed in the action.
- Entrances and exits through the audience can add an extra dimension and possibilities for audience participation.

Cons

- Wherever the performers stand, their backs will always be facing towards one section of the audience. This means it's crucial for them to move around the stage frequently.
- It only allows for minimal scenery — anything too large would ruin the sightlines for someone.

Traverse stages split the audience down the middle

1) A traverse stage is a long, narrow stage that runs straight through the middle of the audience. The actors' position on stage is important as both sections of the audience need to be able to see what's happening.

© Johan Persson / ArenaPAL

A 2014 production of 'The Railway Children' used a traverse stage.

2) Traverse stages are another way of making the audience feel more involved in the action. They bring the audience so close to the performers that it's possible for them to interact.
3) As well as being closer to the action, audience members are closer to each other. When the audience can see each other, it reminds them that they're watching a play — this makes it less realistic.
4) Traverse stages are also difficult to light. Any lighting needs to be placed above the stage to avoid creating shadows on one side.
5) Scenery needs to be designed so that it doesn't distract the audience or block their sightlines. Backdrops can't be used.

Black box studios are flexible performance spaces

1) A black box studio is a room with black walls, a black floor and seating that can be moved around.
2) Black box studios are hugely versatile — they're a blank canvas that can be adapted to meet the needs of different productions. They're also much easier (and cheaper) to build and maintain.
3) Most black box studios are fitted with basic lighting and sound equipment, but any scenery would need to be built from scratch. It can be hard to create different effects in such an empty space.
4) If the seating is all at ground level rather than being raked (where seats are on an upwards slope away from the stage) it can be useful to introduce different levels (see p.18) to the stage. This will make it easier for people at the back of the audience to see what's going on.

Staging

Revolving stages go around in circles

A 2012 production of 'Chariots of Fire' used a revolving stage.

1) Any stage or section of stage that rotates is called a revolving stage (see p.33). Revolving stages were invented to create a smooth transition between scenes, without having to send people on stage to move the scenery and props.
2) However, they're now used to produce a wide range of effects, particularly in plays that are made in more unusual styles.
3) One problem with revolving stages is that they're expensive. They can also pose safety risks for the actors.

Site-specific theatre doesn't take place in a theatre at all

1) Not all productions take place in a theatre. Site-specific theatre is a form of staging which takes somewhere that isn't a theatre and transforms it into a performance space on a temporary basis.
2) For a production to be site-specific, the performance space is often similar to the location in which the play is set. For example, a site-specific production of *Macbeth* might take place in a real castle.
3) Site-specific theatre can be an exciting experience for the audience. It helps the director to create the desired atmosphere, and is often more interactive than traditional theatre as there are fewer barriers between the audience and performers.
4) However, staging a play outside of a theatre isn't always practical. The performance space is unlikely to be well-equipped, so every aspect of the set design would need to be brought in from elsewhere.

Promenade theatre gets audience members on their feet

1) In promenade theatre, the performance space constantly changes — rather than sitting down for the whole performance, the audience is expected to follow the performers between multiple 'stages'.
2) Promenade theatre usually takes place outdoors, so it depends on the weather like other open-air theatres. It's possible to do it indoors, but only if the performance space is large enough.
3) Sharing the same space as the performers is an engaging experience for the audience, but it also makes promenade theatre quite unpredictable. It's difficult to rehearse if you don't know how different audiences are going to behave.
4) Immersive theatre productions (see p.14) often use site-specific or promenade staging. The audience might be more engaged with a performance that doesn't take place in a theatre — the variety of settings makes the production more interesting and unusual. However, the audience might get tired if they have to move around and there could be extra health and safety risks.

Punchdrunk

Punchdrunk is a theatre company with its own twist on promenade theatre. The audience is invited to move freely between different performance spaces instead of being told when to go where.

Time to revise like it's going out of fashion...

Write a paragraph about the staging of a production that you've seen recently. Make sure you answer all of the following questions:

1) Which stage configuration did the production use?
2) What effect did the staging have on the audience?
3) Would you have used the same staging if you were the director? Why / why not?

Tick list:
✓ technical terminology
✓ effect on the audience
✓ advantages and disadvantages

Spaces on Stage

What good is a stage if you don't know where to stand? If only there was a page to explain it all for you...

Different positions on stage have different names

1) Whether you're writing about a play or producing it, you need to use technical terminology to describe different stage positions. This helps to avoid confusion over which part of the stage you're talking about.
2) Stage position can tell the audience more about the characters, as well as their relationships (see p.26).
3) Take a look at the diagram below. Remember — stage positions are named from the actor's perspective:

BACKSTAGE

Wings	Upstage Right (USR)	Upstage Centre (USC)	Upstage Left (USL)	Wings
	Stage Right (SR)	Centre Stage (CS)	Stage Left (SL)	
	Downstage Right (DSR)	Downstage Centre (DSC)	Downstage Left (DSL)	

AUDIENCE

The wings serve as a waiting area for the performers.

They're also used to store props and scenery.

These terms are for a proscenium arch stage (p.15). For other stages, one direction is chosen as 'downstage' and the rest of the terms use this as a reference.

There's more than one way to enter and exit the stage...

1) There are several different ways of getting on and off the stage — these are called entrances and exits.
2) The most common way to enter and exit the stage is through the wings, but not all stage configurations have these. If this is the case, the performers may need to use walkways leading through the audience.
3) In some theatres, other entrances and exits can be used. For example, a performer could appear from under the stage through a trapdoor, or they could even be attached to cables and lowered to the stage.
4) The director needs to consider the dramatic effect of these different options. They can tell the audience more about the character entering or exiting, or contribute to the mood by creating humour or tension.

... and it can be split into multiple levels

1) Most stages are all on the same level, but it's also possible to have multiple levels to a stage — this is called split staging.
2) Some larger theatres are built with split staging, but the same effect can also be created with raised platforms called rostra.
3) Split staging is a versatile technique. It can be used to reflect a change in time or location, but only if it's made clear to the audience. Otherwise, there's a chance it'll just confuse them.
4) Another use of split staging is to separate characters from each other. For example, characters could be placed at different heights to reflect a difference in social class between them.

The Globe Theatre has a built-in gallery above the main stage.

Upstage the rest by using all the right lingo...

The sooner you get in the habit of using technical terminology, the better your answers will be in the exam. If you're not speaking the same language, it'll be hard to get your amazing ideas across to the examiner.

Revision Summary

That was an awful lot of information, so have a go at these questions to make sure it's all gone in.

- Try these questions and tick off each one when you get it right.
- When you've done all the questions for a topic and are completely happy with it, tick off the topic.

Roles of Theatre Makers (p.2-3)

1) Give three tasks that are the responsibility of the play's director.
2) Name two types of designers and describe the work that they do.

Theatre in Context (p.4-5)

3) What three categories can context be divided into?
4) Why are Shakespeare's plays so well-suited to modern interpretations?

Form and Genre (p.6-7)

5) What is meant by the term 'catharsis'?
6) How are modern tragic heroes different to the heroes of Greek tragedies?
7) Give three characteristics of a comedy.

Dramatic Structure (p.8-9)

8) Name all five parts in the dramatic structure of a five-act play.
9) Why might a director choose to use an episodic structure?
10) Give one alternative to a linear plot and describe its effect.

Conventions of Theatre (p.10-11)

11) Give three uses for stage directions in modern theatre.
12) What is the difference between a monologue and a soliloquy?
13) Give three ways in which dramatic irony can be created.

Style (p.12-14)

14) Name the style of theatre associated with each of the following theatre practitioners:
    a) Konstantin Stanislavski
    b) Bertolt Brecht
    c) Antonin Artaud
15) What is the fourth wall?
16) Give one common criticism of naturalism.
17) Describe the role of the audience in forum theatre.

Staging (p.15-17)

18) Give one advantage and one disadvantage of a proscenium arch stage.
19) What was the original purpose of revolving stages?
20) Explain what makes a theatre production site-specific.

Spaces on Stage (p.18)

21) Whose perspective are the stage positions named from?
22) Give one reason a director might choose to use split staging.

Characterisation

Characters are more than just the words they say — an actor's performance helps them spring into life.

Characters are brought to life through characterisation

1) Characterisation is the way an actor interprets and performs their character.
2) Actors may spend many hours researching their role and developing it during rehearsals (see p.23). They'll use the dialogue and stage directions in the script, as well as their own thoughts and interpretations.
3) Characterisation is created partly by the playwright (some aspects will usually be the same from production to production), and partly by the performer. Theatre makers will use the specific features of their production, such as its style, staging and context, to make sure each character is performed in a way that suits their interpretation of the play.
4) The characterisation of a role is often influenced by the director's interpretation of the play's message. Directors may instruct a performer to characterise their role in a certain way to highlight the message or subtext of the play.
5) Characterisation has an impact on the audience — a performer needs to consider what kind of response they want the audience to have towards their character, e.g. fear, admiration, sympathy. This will shape how they perform their role.

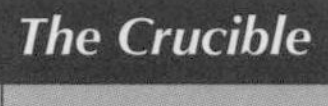

The Crucible

Some aspects of John Proctor's character are likely to be the same across different productions because his age, build and personality traits are all described in the script. However, a performer can choose to perform his character in a way that brings out different sides of his personality. For example, an actor could emphasise his guilty and flawed side, or play him as more confident and self-assured. This can be done using an actor's physical and vocal performance skills.

A character's backstory is important

1) A character's backstory is made up of all the things that have happened to them before the action of the play begins.
2) The audience can learn about a character's backstory through what others say, what the character says or through flashbacks. Actors can also learn about their character's backstory through stage directions.
3) The theatre maker Stanislavski (see p.12) felt that actors should understand their character's backstory and how it affects their character's motivations as it can explain why they might act in a particular way. It makes the actor's performance and reactions much more convincing, which in turn helps the audience to suspend their disbelief.
4) A character's backstory can generate sympathy from the audience, e.g. in *Hamlet*, an audience may see Hamlet's treatment of Ophelia differently after learning that his beloved father was murdered.

Kenneth Branagh and Kate Winslet in 'Hamlet'.

Context is part of characterisation

1) It's important to take historical and social context into account when considering characterisation.
2) The way a character acts or reacts is likely to be influenced by when and where the play is set. Context shapes how different people were expected to behave according to their gender, race or class.
3) Context is also important for explaining different relationships within the play. For example, Arthur Birling treats his wife and daughter differently to the men in *An Inspector Calls* (set in 1912), whereas there's no distinction between male and female characters in *DNA* (set roughly in the early 2000s).
4) Context also affects the social status of characters within the play. For example, in *The Crucible*, Tituba is a victim of the racist attitudes of the characters, which is part of the play's 17th-century context.

Characterisation

Most plays have a protagonist and an antagonist

Eliza Doolittle in a 2010 production of 'Pygmalion'.

1) A character's status in a narrative is likely to influence an actor's performance. The protagonist and the antagonist have important roles in making the audience feel emotionally involved in the action as well as moving the plot forwards.
2) The protagonist is the main character, and the plot follows their experiences and character development. Protagonists are typically the 'hero'.
3) Protagonists tend to have some admirable or relatable personality traits, e.g. Eliza Doolittle in *Pygmalion* is likeable and intelligent. Protagonists often develop during the play, although not always for the better (see p.22).
4) Most protagonists aren't perfect — for example, they may be an 'anti-hero' (a hero with obvious character flaws). Character flaws can make it easier for an audience to relate to a protagonist because they seem more realistic and human.
5) The antagonist is the character who causes trouble for the protagonist — they're usually disliked by an audience. The antagonist's character often doesn't develop in the same way a protagonist does, e.g. in *Othello*, Iago is evil and manipulative throughout the play and doesn't change or grow.

Supporting and minor characters create interest

1) Every role in a play has a purpose, including supporting or minor characters. Actors playing these parts need to use performance skills to create characters in-keeping with the play's style and setting.
2) Supporting characters are an important part of the plot, but they're not the audience's main focus, e.g. Linda in *Blood Brothers*. They may have a relationship with the protagonist or antagonist, or be part of the play's narrative.

Comic Relief

Some minor characters exist for comic effect. Minor characters in many of Shakespeare's plays, such as the Porter in *Macbeth*, offer the audience light relief between more tense scenes.

3) Minor characters are those that generally have little impact on the plot, but they're important for making the world of the play more interesting and believable. They may also be useful for setting the tone of a scene. For example, in *Blood Brothers*, the Milkman refuses to give Mrs Johnstone any milk because of unpaid bills, helping to create a sense of injustice as well as sympathy for Mrs Johnstone.
4) Although many minor characters only have background roles, they can often reveal more about the main characters through the way the main character treats them or speaks to them.

Stock characters are instantly recognisable

A stereotype's characteristics can be oversimplified so they don't seem realistic.

1) A stock character is recognised by an audience as a stereotype. Stock characters include the damsel in distress, wicked witch, mad scientist or gentle giant.
2) Playwrights may use stock characters as a quick way of making sure the audience understands that character. The audience will already be familiar with that 'type' of character from books, films and other plays and they will have certain expectations about how that character will behave.
3) Playwrights can use what seem like stock characters to surprise an audience by undermining their assumptions. Introducing a stock character who doesn't conform to the audience's expectations can be used for comic effect or to criticise a stereotype by making an audience challenge their prejudices.

EXAM TIP

Plays set underground — full of miner characters...

In the exam, you'll need to show that you've considered how characterisation is developed by actors. They'll use the character's backstory and role in the narrative to create an impact on the audience.

Characterisation

To be believable (and interesting) for audiences, most characters need to develop in some way.

Some characters change and develop during a play

1) The way a character changes from the start to the end of a play is called their 'character arc'.
2) A protagonist's character arc often has a dramatic effect and drives the play's narrative. Their character draws the audience into the plot — the audience is interested in seeing the protagonist overcome their flaws or challenges, which in turn can create tension and suspense.
3) The development of a character arc may teach the audience something. Some theatre makers, such as Brecht (see p.12), use character arcs to communicate a moral message to the audience. They might use a character's development to influence how they'd like to change the audience's opinions.
4) Here's an example of a character arc for Elizabeth Proctor in *The Crucible*:

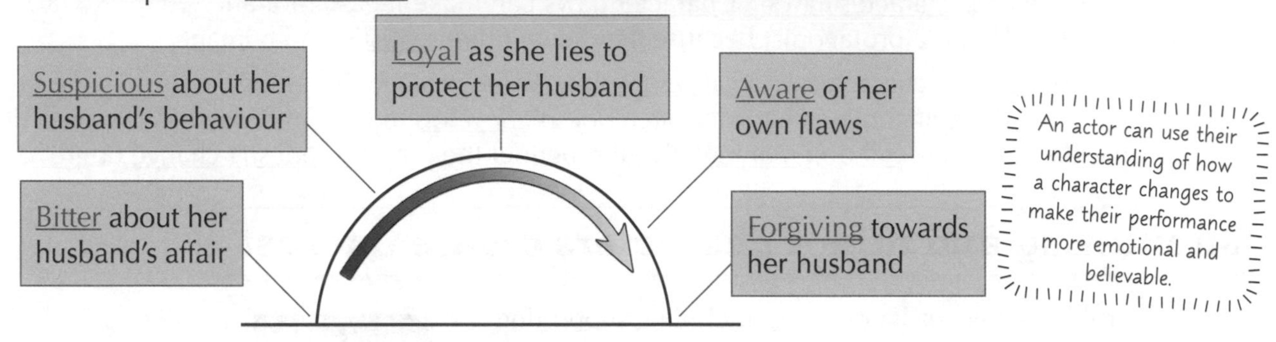

Some protagonists change to overcome challenges...

1) The protagonist's character arc can be part of the play's resolution (see p.8).
2) Overcoming obstacles and challenges in order to reach a goal is often part of character development.
3) A protagonist might have to deal with obstacles such as:
   - The antagonist's actions, e.g. spreading lies about the protagonist.
   - Tragic circumstances, e.g. war, natural disaster or illness.
   - A protagonist's own flaws, e.g. stubbornness, pride or jealousy.
4) At the end of a comedy, there's often a sense of resolution or relief that the protagonist has overcome the difficulties they faced and become stronger or wiser as a result. This creates a satisfying ending for the audience.

In 'Much Ado About Nothing', Benedick must overcome his pride before he can get married.

... but some protagonists struggle to change for the better

1) When a protagonist doesn't change or learn from their mistakes, it can have tragic consequences. It can lead a protagonist to make a choice which brings about their downfall or death.
2) If the protagonist fails to change or adapt to circumstances, the audience may get a sense of tragic inevitability that the events in the play won't be resolved. This means that a tense and uneasy atmosphere looms over much of the play because the audience suspect that there won't be a happy ending.
3) A character might even change for the worse as a result of the actions of the play. This could be because they are struggling with feelings such as guilt or remorse. For example, in *DNA*, characters respond differently to guilt — Leah leaves the group, whereas Phil withdraws further into himself. The play doesn't finish with neatly resolved character arcs — it leaves the audience with lots of questions.

Characterisation

Relationships with other characters are important

1) The audience can learn a lot about a character from the way they interact with others. This might be a short interaction with a minor character or a key relationship which drives the narrative of the play.
2) All relationships on stage tell the audience something. Relationships can show family ties (e.g. mother and son), social bonds (e.g. neighbours) or less formal connections (e.g. colleagues or acquaintances).
3) Relationships can dictate a character's status within the play, e.g. a parent would usually have a higher status than their child within a family group. If there is an inequality in a character relationship because of a difference in power, social status or gender, this can create tension and interest for the audience.
4) Relationships can be complex and are likely to change throughout the play — like the protagonist's character arc, they often drive the play's narrative and are a source of dramatic tension.
5) The beginning or end of a relationship can have a strong impact on the audience, especially if it involves the protagonist. For example, there may be suspense and good humour when a relationship is developing, whereas conflict and tension are more likely when a relationship breaks down.

Foils

A foil is a character who contrasts with the protagonist. Their similarities and differences highlight the good or bad characteristics of the protagonist. In *Death of a Salesman*, Charley is successful and happy, making him a foil to Willy (the play's unhappy protagonist).

Rehearsals can shape characterisation

Rehearsal techniques can develop a performer's understanding of a character by allowing them to get in touch with their character's personality and motivations.

There are more exercises to help with character development on p.45.

- Method acting: when a performer fully immerses themselves in their role and aims to become their character, both on stage and off stage.
- Hot-seating: an actor in the 'hot seat' is asked questions by the rest of the cast and they must answer in role as their character. This can help the actor to imagine how their character would react in different situations.
- Status games: it's important for a performer to understand their relationships with other characters. Arranging the cast into a tableau, using levels and space to indicate high and low status characters and their relationship to one another, can show how different characters might treat each other.
- Defend a character: this involves pretending to be a character's lawyer and defending them from accusations from the rest of the cast about an error they've made within the play. The actor could find examples that excuse or justify their actions, and show that characters aren't simply good or evil.

A tableau is when the action stops and the characters freeze in position.

If your stimulus is a balloon, don't forget tableau it up...

Find a photo in a newspaper of someone whose identity you don't know. Imagine that you are developing a character using the photo as a stimulus, then write a paragraph about them, answering the following questions:

1) What is the character's backstory?
2) What qualities does the character have?
3) What are the character's important relationships?

Tick list:
✓ how characterisation is created
✓ types of characters
✓ relationships on stage

Physical Performance Skills

Have a look at these pages on physical performance — take your time though, it doesn't need to be a sprint...

Physical performance creates an impact on the audience

1) An actor's physical performance builds up a visual impression of their character for the audience.
2) This visual impression could include the character's age, build, height, facial features, movement, posture, mannerisms and facial expressions.
3) A character's appearance on stage is likely to be partly based on details from the text. Other details are created by the director and the performer's interpretation, so will vary from production to production.
4) An actor may be cast by the director because their appearance matches the physical aspects of the role. However, an actor still needs to use their performance skills to create an appropriate 'physicality' (physical stage presence) for their character.

Age, build and height are key aspects of characterisation

1) Age, build and height are important aspects of character, alongside others like gender, race and personality.
2) These features are usually taken into consideration when casting actors, but they can be reinforced through posture, movement and stage presence. They can also be created through effective use of costume and make-up (see p.38-39).
3) Some playwrights give information about these aspects of character in their stage directions or imply them in dialogue.
4) Other playwrights may leave things open to interpretation. For example, in Dennis Kelly's *DNA*, minimal information is given about the characters, and their appearance and gender can be changed for different productions. This suggests that the appearance of the character is less important than their actions.

Age

Younger characters could be shown through energetic and restless movements. An older character may be frail and less dynamic so they may move more slowly.

Build

An actor could make themselves appear broader by using a confident stance and strong posture. In contrast, graceful movements could make a character seem dainty.

Height

Using an upright posture can allow an actor to make their character seem taller, while a slumped or hunched posture can make a character seem smaller.

Movement and stillness can be effective

1) The way an actor moves on stage can tell the audience about their character. A proud person may stride confidently onto centre stage, whereas a nervous one might shuffle hesitantly to the side.
2) Specific movements can be used to show a character's reaction to something. For example, if a character leaps quickly to their feet, this could show desperation or excitement. Depending on the context, this tells the audience about their inner thoughts or reactions.
3) Stillness can also have a significant impact. A lack of movement or reaction could indicate something about their character, e.g. Phil in *DNA* sometimes doesn't react at all, showing he has a sense of calmness or even a complete lack of empathy. Being still and calm in unusual situations can be shocking to an audience.

Antony Sher as Willy Loman in a 2005 production of 'Death of a Salesman'.

Physical Performance Skills

Body language adds depth to a character

1) Body language is a type of non-verbal communication — an actor can use movements, facial expressions and posture to communicate how a character is thinking or feeling.
2) For example, if a character crosses their arms when speaking to another character, this creates a physical barrier, suggesting there is something they don't like about the other. If a character speaks to another character with arms open, they come across as being friendly and welcoming.
3) Posture (how a performer sits and stands) is an aspect of body language:

- An upright posture could imply that a character is confident or relaxed.
- A slouched posture could suggest that a character is inward-looking, lazy or lacking in confidence.
- Leaning back can be used to emphasise a character's laugh or show that they are recoiling from something. It can also hint that the character is holding something back and is being secretive.
- Leaning forward can be used to show a character is curious about something or they have a hidden interest in the events.

© Nigel Norrington / ArenaPAL

These actors show their characters' affection for one another by using body language.

Gesture is the way actors move their body

1) Gestures are movements created with parts of the body, such as the hands, arms and head. Some gestures are obvious, such as a nod or pointing at something. Subtle gestures can also be important, such as a slightly inclined head or shoulder shrug.
2) A gesture is an effective way of demonstrating a character's emotions, e.g. throwing their arms in the air could show shock or excitement.
3) Mannerisms are small, repeated gestures — these can bring out aspects of a character's personality.
4) For example, a character repeatedly touching their face could suggest nervousness or unease, while a character who often yawns frequently could be lazy or indifferent.

Mime

Mime uses movement to create meaning. An actor will use actions and gestures instead of using dialogue or props.

A character's face shows their reactions

1) A character's emotional reaction to an event or other characters is revealed through their facial expressions.
2) Facial expressions are movements of the eyes, eyebrows and mouth, such as smiling or frowning.
3) Actors need to consider whether the audience can see subtle facial expressions. An actor might exaggerate their expressions slightly so they're more obvious — but they must be careful not to go over the top (unless exaggeration is part of the characterisation, such as for a pantomime dame).
4) Facial expressions can either emphasise what a character says or contradict it, e.g. a sly smile could indicate that a character isn't being truthful when making a promise.
5) Facial expressions are recognisable to an audience because they're used in everyday life to show emotions. The audience can recognise different degrees of despair, happiness, anger, fear or surprise because they're realistic. This helps the audience to relate to how the characters on stage are feeling.

Gestures — they're always a bit of a juggling act...

When writing about how an actor might create a response from an audience, you should think about what effect their movements create — almost every movement that an actor makes is deliberate.

Physical Performance — Interactions and Spacing

Physical performance skills are needed for interacting with other characters on stage too — ooh err...

Physical performance involves other characters

1) Relationships between characters are shown by the way characters interact on stage — this interaction is often based on physical performance.
2) As relationships change and develop during a play, so does each character's physical performance. It gives the audience clues about their relationship.
3) There are many different ways for actors to develop their characters' relationships, including things like eye contact, grouping, onstage location and proxemics.

Brick and Maggie showing distance in a 2017 production of 'Cat on a Hot Tin Roof'.

Proxemics is the space between characters

1) Proxemics refers to the physical space between actors on stage. It's one of the most obvious ways of showing relationships.
2) Characters who are physically close on stage could be in agreement or linked in some way. If characters become more distant on stage, this could suggest their relationship is less close or they don't agree on something.
3) A performer can use proxemics to show relationships becoming weaker or stronger, or to create tension.
4) Proxemics is used alongside the context of the rest of the play, e.g. two characters who are close on stage could be romantically linked or they could be about to fight.
5) Another important aspect of stage space is blocking — this is closely linked to proxemics:

- Blocking refers to the process of planning the positions and movements of actors on stage to ensure the audience has the best line of sight for the key points in a production. Blocking is planned during rehearsals by the director to make sure the audience can see everything properly.
- In order for an audience to fully understand the effect of proxemics, it's important that they have a clear view of the spacing of characters on stage.
- Blocking ensures the physical performance and interactions between characters have the intended dramatic effect. It's a key part of the relationship between performer and audience.

A character's location on stage is important

See p.18 for the names of the different stage positions.

1) The location of characters on the stage is important and affects the relationship between the performers and the audience.
2) Character location shows which characters are important and who the audience should focus on. For example, if a character is downstage, the audience is more likely to pay attention to them. This makes the character seem more important than a character who is upstage and who the audience is less likely to be watching.
3) A character who is standing more centrally on stage might also seem more important to the audience than a character standing to one side of the stage.

The Audience

It's important for actors to think about what the audience can see. An actor might face another character to show a connection between them, but be slightly tilted towards the audience so the audience can still see their facial expressions and body language.

Physical Performance — Interactions and Spacing

Grouping is an aspect of proxemics

© Joan Marcus / ArenaPAL

In this scene from 'Blood Brothers', the Narrator is detached from the action so he stands slightly apart from the group.

1) Grouping is the deliberate decision for an actor to place themselves close to a group of characters on stage. Grouping is important for creating meaning as it gives the audience a visual clue to relationships and alliances between characters.
2) By attaching themselves to a group, part of an actor's character is revealed, e.g. their character may admire the traits of the group, or they may be weak or timid and use the group for a sense of security.
3) A character's place within a group is important. An actor standing in the middle of a group might show that they are a leader or are important to the other characters. A character on the edge of the group could be a follower or outsider.

Eye contact shows a connection between characters

1) Making and breaking eye contact is a simple but powerful part of physical performance.
2) Eye contact can set up a connection between characters, show intensity within their relationship or reveal a shared thought or agreement. Eye contact could last a moment or be more sustained.
3) Repeated 'stolen' glances at another character can suggest a character is infatuated with them.
4) A lack of eye contact can show a bad relationship, disagreement or a lack of respect. Breaking eye contact can show that what a character is saying or doing isn't sincere.
5) Being unable to maintain eye contact could also be a character trait which suggests a feeling of nervousness or insecurity.

Blood Brothers

The actor playing Mrs Lyons may fail to keep eye contact when she lies to Mrs Johnstone about the superstition that separated twins will die if they ever learn that they were once a pair.

How a character reacts to others is important

1) The way a character behaves when they're not speaking can tell the audience a lot about them.
2) Active listening is when an actor reacts in character to what is happening on stage. Doing this in a believable way helps to show the character's personality.
3) Active listening is most effective when an actor has a good understanding of their character's motivations.

Naturalism

Stanislavski believed an actor should understand their character's motivations — he thought that characters should be as believable as possible (see p.12).

Active listening — the latest fitness craze...

Choose a key scene from a play you're studying. Write down your own stage directions that you might use if you were to act it out. You should consider:

1) How proxemics could be used to show relationships between different characters.
2) Blocking and characters' locations on stage.
3) Use of eye contact to show meaning.

Tick list:
- ✓ proxemics
- ✓ blocking and stage positioning
- ✓ interactions with others

Vocal Performance Skills

Dialogue is just words on a page until actors bring it to life on the stage using their vocal skills.

Actors need to express themselves

1) Vocal performance (the way an actor speaks their lines) is just as important as the lines themselves — it can create meaning and character.
2) The way an actor creates a character's voice tells an audience about a character's emotional state, as well as their status, background and personality.
3) Vocal performance adds meaning to a character's words — it might show they are being sarcastic, insincere or persuading someone to do something.
4) The way that characters speak to each other can build up meaning about relationships, e.g. whether they are close or distant, loving or hostile.
5) Vocal performance can also show how a character changes through the play — as a character develops, an actor may adjust their performance to reflect this, for example, using a slower, more evenly-paced delivery as their character ages.

© Nigel Norrington / ArenaPAL

An actor playing Lady Bracknell in 'The Importance of Being Earnest' could speak loudly and forcefully.

Accents can provide background information

1) A character's accent signals where they're from to an audience.
2) Accents can indicate a character's social class and status. Received Pronunciation can show that a character is upper class, whereas a regional accent could suggest the character is of a working-class background.
3) Differences in accents (and social class) can reflect tensions between characters. For example, in *Blood Brothers*, Edward Lyons is called "a friggin' poshy" so an actor playing him could use Received Pronunciation to reflect this. This would contrast with the Johnstones' Liverpudlian accents.
4) In *An Inspector Calls*, Priestley describes Arthur Birling as being *"provincial in his speech"*, meaning he has a regional accent. An actor playing Birling could use a regional accent to highlight the character is middle class, rather than upper class like Gerald Croft.

Received Pronunciation is considered the accent of Standard English in the UK and has the highest social status.

Narrators

If a narrator has an accent which is different to the other characters, they may seem more removed from the action, which could suggest they are impartial.

Volume and pitch are essential vocal skills

1) Volume refers to how loud or quiet a vocal performance is. An actor's volume could be a feature of a character or a reaction to a particular event.
2) A loud voice could show that a character is happy or angry, whereas a soft whisper may suggest fear or nervousness. An audience can tune in very quickly to different types of emotional delivery.
3) Pitch is how high or low an actor's voice is (somewhere in-between is typical). Speaking in a high or low pitch could be a feature of a character that an actor uses all the way through a performance. For example, a high-pitched voice could show that a character is young or naive, whereas a low pitch carries more authority.
4) Pitch can also be used to show a character's emotional state — a high pitch could show excitement or surprise, while a low pitch could show seriousness or sadness.

Projection

It's really important that actors project their voices on stage so that the audience can hear what they are saying. This involves speaking with good diction — diction means pronouncing the words clearly.

Vocal Performance Skills

Pace is the speed that lines are delivered

1) The speed or pace that an actor uses to deliver their lines can also build up a sense of a character. For example:
   - A slow pace can show thoughtfulness, weariness or old age, or indicate that the character is inward-looking, lonely or depressed.
   - An even, regular pace can indicate self-confidence and composure.
   - A fast pace can show youthfulness or nervousness.
2) Meaning can be created by varying pace at important moments, e.g. speeding up delivery so that the words tumble out quickly can be used to show excitement, confusion or an emotional breakdown.
3) The audience will use the context of the spoken words to understand the change of pace — the situation, dialogue and non-verbal communication will show how the words should be interpreted.

© Donald Cooper / photostage

In 'DNA', Brian's lines might be delivered quickly during his mental breakdown.

Pauses can be dramatic

1) An actor can use timing and pauses between each part of dialogue to shape the delivery of their lines.
2) Pauses are useful for creating tension. They give the audience time to reflect on what is happening. Longer periods of silence can also build tension, sometimes to the point where it becomes unbearable for the audience.
3) A dramatic pause could imply that a character is about to reveal an important piece of information.
4) If a character uses pauses frequently, it could show that they're unsure or lacking in confidence.
5) Pauses also help dialogue to seem more realistic — they can suggest that a character is thinking of what to say next, just like in everyday speech.

The Pinter Pause

Harold Pinter (1930-2008) was a playwright who was famous for including dramatic pauses and lengthy periods of silence in his work. These pauses heighten tension or give a feeling of menace in key scenes — they're particularly jarring in scenes where you would expect a reaction or some dialogue.

Phrasing is how speech is naturally broken up

1) Actors use phrasing to break up dialogue into small chunks (phrases). Phrasing makes the dialogue easier to understand and can be used to emphasise any subtext or meaning in the words.
2) Phrases are created by adding pauses in the right places. A 'natural pause' happens when a thought is completed (usually at the end of a sentence). It gives the actor a chance to breathe at the end of a thought rather than breaking the flow of speech partway through.
3) Here's an example of how an actor could use phrasing in an extract from *The Importance of Being Earnest* by Oscar Wilde:

short pause — *longer, natural pause*

JACK: When one is in town one amuses oneself.
When one is in the country one amuses other people.

separate phrases

By separating this dialogue into the underlined phrases, an actor can emphasise the difference between the town and country, which creates comedy.

4) Phrases are also created through intonation (the rise and fall of natural speech) — see p.30 for more.

Subtext

An actor needs to understand the meaning or 'subtext' of the written words of the play to help them create effective phrasing. Creating phrases in the wrong place can be confusing or sound out of place.

Vocal Performance Skills

Intonation and emphasis influence the meaning of a line

1) Intonation is the rise and fall of a voice to create a natural pattern of speech. It can also be used to create meaning, for example, rising intonation at the end of a sentence shows that someone is asking a question.
2) Some words might be stressed to create emphasis — an actor might do this to draw attention to the important words in a line, to convey a certain meaning or to get across how their character is feeling.
3) For example, in Henrik Ibsen's *A Doll's House*, an actor playing Nora could stress certain words (underlined in this extract) to emphasise her determination to leave her husband.

NORA: I have never felt my mind so clear and certain as tonight.

Tone adds emotional impact to spoken words

1) By changing the tone of their voice, an actor can provoke a reaction from an audience, e.g. pity or anger. This can be done through the speed of delivery, or the volume, pitch and intensity of their voice.
2) An actor playing John Proctor in *The Crucible* could use tone to demonstrate the character's emotions at different points in the play:

- In Act Two, Proctor feels helpless when his wife is accused. An actor could use a desperate tone to show his distress.
- At the end of the play, Proctor refuses to give a false confession. An actor could use an adamant, confident tone to show he is determined to act honourably.

John and Elizabeth Proctor in a 2014 production of 'The Crucible'.

The musicality of speech has a powerful effect

1) Not all plays are written in natural speech — some playwrights deliberately use non-naturalistic types of speech, such as verse, rhyme or choral speaking, which isn't meant to mirror realistic speech.
2) This can draw the audience's attention to the fact that they're watching something fictional. These types of speech often have a musicality to them (without actually involving any music).
3) Verse (such as blank verse, often used by Shakespeare) usually has a set rhythm and structure. Verse can have a different rhythm to normal speech, though some types of verse mirror normal speech quite closely.
4) Rhyme gives lines a singsong quality and can make them sound upbeat or even sinister. It can also be used for comedy — forced rhymes can be a source of humour if they are emphasised by the actor.
5) Ancient Greek theatre traditionally used choral speech (a group of actors speaking at the same time). Massed voices speaking in unison can be used to comment on the play's action, similar to a narrator.

REVISION TASK

Some plays are in verse — what a treat to rehearse...

Write a paragraph about how an actor used their voice effectively in a performance that you've seen recently. Make sure you cover all of the following points:

1) The techniques the actor used.
2) How the techniques were used to create meaning.
3) How the performance might have been different if the actor had used different techniques.

Tick list:
- ✓ accent
- ✓ volume, pitch and pace
- ✓ pauses and timing to create an effect

Revision Summary

That's it for Section Two — have a go at these questions to recap what you've learnt about characterisation and performance skills.

- Try these questions and tick off each one when you get it right.
- When you've done all the questions for a topic and are completely happy with it, tick off the topic.

Characterisation (p.20-23) ☐

1) Explain what is meant by 'characterisation'. ☐
2) Why is context important for understanding relationships between characters? ☐
3) Give two examples of how a typical protagonist is different from a typical antagonist. ☐
4) Give three examples of types of stock characters. ☐
5) What is meant by the term 'character arc'? ☐
6) Give two examples of obstacles a protagonist might face. ☐
7) What is meant by the term 'foil'? ☐
8) Describe one rehearsal technique an actor might use to get to know their character. ☐

Physical Performance Skills (p.24-25) ☐

9) How do playwrights give information about a character's appearance? ☐
10) Describe an effect that an actor's stillness can have on the audience. ☐
11) Name three aspects of body language. ☐
12) How can an actor's facial expressions convey meaning? ☐

Physical Performance — Interactions and Spacing (p.26-27) ☐

13) What is meant by the term 'proxemics'? ☐
14) Why is blocking important? ☐
15) Describe the effect on the audience if a character is...
    a) upstage centre
    b) downstage right ☐
16) Give an example of a character's positioning in a group and describe the effect it has. ☐
17) How can an actor use active listening to make their character more believable? ☐

Vocal Performance Skills (p.28-30) ☐

18) Name two things a character's accent might tell the audience about their background. ☐
19) How could an actor use pitch to show how a character is feeling? ☐
20) How can pauses be used to create tension? ☐
21) Explain why an actor might stress certain words in a line. ☐
22) What might an actor do to change the tone of their voice? ☐
23) Describe one way that a playwright can create musicality in speech. ☐

Sets

Set designers are responsible for the physical environment on stage, from the props to the backdrops...

The set is usually the first thing an audience sees

1) The set is everything that's visible on stage, including scenery, furniture and props.
2) The set helps the audience to understand what a performance is about even before anything's happened.
3) Effective set design creates meaning and helps the smooth running of the performance.

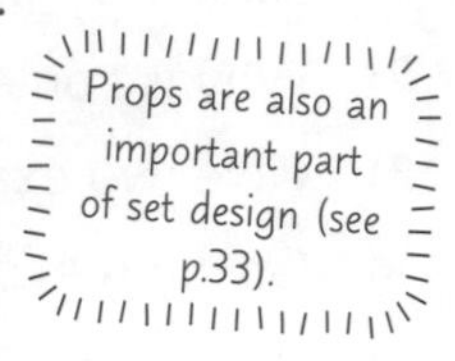

Sets Can Create Meaning By...

- Establishing the location and time period of the production
- Creating mood and atmosphere
- Creating symbolism
- Contributing to the overall visual style of the production

Sets May Also Have To...

- Have enough exits and entrances
- Have different staging levels
- Allow actors enough space to move around the stage
- Give the audience clear sightlines
- Allow for quick scene changes

Set design is part of a production's overall style

See p.12-14 for a reminder on different styles of theatre.

The style of set is its overall 'feel' or look. Here are three of the main styles a production might use:

Naturalistic Sets

- This type of set aims to create the illusion of real life for the audience.
- They're often detailed, using well-researched period furniture and realistic decoration.

Minimalist Sets

- These sets use few props and minimal scenery.
- The audience has to use their imagination more.
- Props are important to symbolise themes or show the time period.

Abstract Sets

- This type of set doesn't try to recreate real life.
- The design doesn't have to be basic — it could be very elaborate.
- They often bring out the play's symbols or themes.

A set designer works closely with the director and other designers to ensure the set fits the production's overall visual style. They could use sketches and model sets to develop their ideas before building them.

Scale, colour and texture are key features of sets

Set designers consider every aspect of physical stage space, such as:

1) Size and shape of stage — sets need to make the best use of space, using levels, entrances and exits in a way that works for the script and for audience sightlines. Stage shape also affects set design, e.g. a piece of set that works well on a proscenium stage might block sightlines in the round.

Composite Sets

Composite sets show several locations on stage at the same time. They can be useful for avoiding multiple scene changes.

2) Scale of sets — the size of the set in the performance space can have a big impact. A small set on a large stage could create a deliberately sparse effect. A large set on a small stage could be overwhelming.
3) Materials and textures — shiny, smooth textures might suggest a modern or urban setting. Ragged cloth and wood could create an impression of a rural setting or a specific historical period.
4) Colour — depending on performance style, colour might be used in a naturalistic way or to add symbolism and decoration to an abstract set. The meaning of colour to audiences depends on context (e.g. a play's themes). Red often suggests danger or passion, and white can mean innocence and purity. Blue can convey calmness or a link to water, and green might symbolise envy or nature.

Sets

Technical equipment can simplify set design

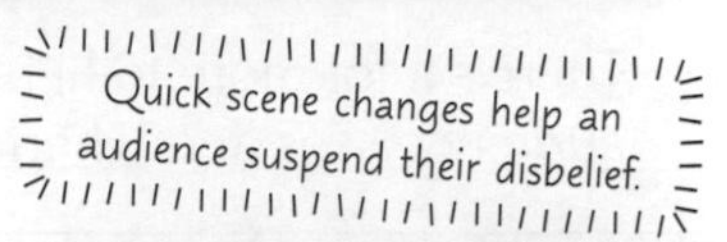

Technical equipment can help a production run more smoothly:

1) Revolving stages are built into some theatres. They're expensive, but make for very speedy scene changes (see p.17) and can create some unusual effects.
2) Trucks are a low-tech way of speeding up scene changes. They're wooden structures on wheels. They've got two faces and can be turned to show either side (e.g. a marble fireplace on one and a grisly dungeon on the other).
3) Projecting images onto a backdrop can be just as effective as constructed scenery. They speed up scene changes since nothing on stage needs moving.
4) Flats (wooden frames with canvas stretched over them) can be painted and used to hide the wings. They can be turned around to show different scenes.
5) Other features of set design create special effects on stage:

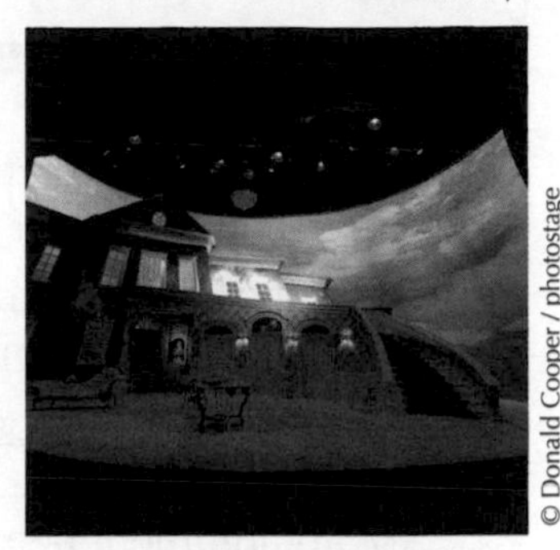

A cyclorama used to create a sky backdrop.

- Multimedia, such as moving images and video, can show things like flashbacks.
- Flying rigs allow actors to 'fly' on invisible wires — this is often used in productions of *Peter Pan*. They can also fly scenery items into place to speed up scene changes.
- A cyclorama is a curved screen which acts as the stage's back wall. Images and light are projected onto it to create a backdrop, e.g. a clear blue sky.
- Smoke machines release a water-based mist mixture into the air. They're a simple way of adding atmosphere, e.g. creating a foggy, mysterious setting.
- Pyrotechnics are stage fireworks. They create special effects (e.g. loud bangs, showers of sparks and flashes of light), but it's important to use them safely.

Props communicate details to the audience

1) A prop is anything moveable on stage which isn't part of the scenery, costumes or cast.
2) Set designers can tell an audience about a play's era and location through individual props, e.g. school desks and a blackboard would help to convey that *The History Boys* is set in a grammar school in the 1980s.
3) Personal props are props used by actors to add depth to their character. An actor's behaviour with the prop tells the audience about the character. For example, a character always keeping a picture of their family with them suggests to the audience they're sentimental. Personal props also tell an audience details like status, e.g. a gold pocket watch suggests a higher social status.
4) Actors should rehearse with their props to get comfortable using them.

Stage Furniture

- Stage furniture is a moveable part of the set which isn't a personal prop, e.g. a clock or a vase.
- Set designers use stage furniture to tell the audience about setting, time and mood.
- Designers will research social and historical context to get the details right and to make sure every piece of stage furniture adds to the overall visual style of the production.

Props to you for getting through this page...

This stuff is a mix of common sense and theatrical terms, but it's all useful to know for the exam. The really important thing is to always be thinking about how design choices affect the audience's experience.

Lighting

There's a lot more to lighting design than pressing an on-switch. Lighting plays a big part in what the audience sees and when they see it, but designers can also use their lights to alter how action is perceived.

Lighting helps to control what the audience sees

1) Lighting has a practical purpose in plays — it focuses the audience's attention on a particular character or part of the stage. This helps to emphasise important moments, actors or dialogue.
2) Lighting can also communicate the time of day and location — the lighting in an evening forest scene might be dim and greenish, but would be bright white on a tropical beach at noon.
3) It also creates atmosphere and tension in a scene, e.g. gradually increasing brightness over the course of an argument between two characters will help to increase the emotional intensity of the scene.
4) Absence of light can be just as useful. Blackouts and fades indicate scene changes to the audience and let set and stage furniture changes happen without being too disruptive to the action.

Light sources need to fit with the play's style. In a naturalistic play, onstage light sources should be right for the play's setting to help the audience suspend their disbelief. In an abstract performance, the designer might use strange or surreal light effects to increase the sense of spectacle.

Lighting creates dramatic possibilities

Intensity, colour and direction can create dramatic lighting effects.

In this 2010 production of 'The Tempest', an intense blue downlight represents the sea and creates a cold mood.

Intensity

1) In stage lighting, 'intensity' is a light's brightness.
2) Harder (or brighter) light can make a scene feel more emotionally intense. It creates more distinct shadows and is more dramatic.
3) Softer (or dimmer) light reduces the amount of shadow and makes for a less intense stage picture and a less dramatic mood.

Colour

1) Colour symbolism is a really important aspect of lighting design.
2) Colour can also show time of day and location, e.g. a night-time scene might use pale violet light to give the impression of moonlight, or blue-green light could be used to suggest a location near water.
3) Lighting designers can use colour to change the on-stage mood, e.g. orange light would bring out warmer colours in scenery and costumes, and blue light would make the colours and mood colder.

Direction

1) Lighting the stage from different directions can create effects for the audience. Lighting can highlight parts of the stage or create shadows. Shadows can be made darker or added in strange places.
2) Lighting a scene from the front is the most common arrangement for proscenium arch stages. It looks natural, with enough shade to define the actors but without casting too many shadows.
3) Downlighting (lighting from above) is also fairly common. The nearer the lantern is to being directly over an actor on the stage, the more strange shadows will be cast over their face and body.
4) Uplighting (lighting from below) casts shadows over actors' faces, especially their eyes which can appear to the audience as dark pits in their face. It's useful for lighting tense or unsettling scenes.

Lighting

There are three main stage lanterns

Health and safety is really important in lighting, and in stage design generally (see p.53).

Stage lights are called lanterns. They're held above the stage by the lighting rig. Different lanterns have different purposes:

1) Profile spotlights cast sharply defined beams. They can precisely focus light on specific actors or parts of the stage. When they're used with gobos, they can project shapes and images onto the stage (see below).
2) Fresnel spotlights (pronounced 'frennel') cast softer-edged beams than profile spotlights, so they're good for mingling with other lighting effects, like floodlights. Their beams can be shaped using barndoors (see below).
3) Floodlights light large areas like backcloths or cycloramas. They're good for wide washes of colour, e.g. they can be arranged in blocks with different coloured tints to create dawn and dusk effects.

© Donald Cooper / photostage

Lighting can be used to focus the audience's attention on a performer.

Specialised lanterns create unusual effects

1) Parcans are powerful lanterns that can have their beam angle set to illuminate very wide or very narrow areas. Using multiple parcans is great for making deeply coloured washes of light in many colours at once, e.g. they could be used to provide authentic, atmospheric lighting in a scene at a rock concert.
2) Strobes create flashes of very bright light at fast regular intervals. Used on their own, strobes can make the action appear to be in slow motion — they're good for things like dream sequences.

Manipulating light also makes special effects

Here are a few more ways designers use light to create effects:

1) Focusing a lantern's white light through gels (heat-resistant, coloured plastic filters) can change its colour. Gels can be bought in a variety of colours that can be combined to make a huge range of shades and tints.
2) Gobos are thin metal discs with patterns or pictures cut out of them. They're slotted into a profile spotlight to project an image onto a backdrop or the stage, e.g. a castle wall or light shining through a tree's leaves.
3) Barndoors are hinged metal flaps attached to the front of a lantern. They can be angled in different ways to block light from parts of the stage.
4) Lighting designers can use a bright backlight (light from behind performers) to make silhouettes of the actors on stage. If they do the same thing with a screen in front of the performers, they can make shadow theatre.

© Donald Cooper / photostage

Gobos can be used to create a dappled leaf effect.

There's nothing like a bit of light reading...

Write a paragraph about the use of lighting in a scene of a play that you've seen recently. Make sure you answer all of the following questions:

1) What sort of lighting equipment was used in the play?
2) How did the lighting impact on the mood?
3) How did the lighting designer use light to tell the audience about time and place?

Tick list:
✓ effect on audience
✓ details about equipment and techniques
✓ creation of meaning

Sound

The sound designer's role will vary in scope depending on the size and type of a production. There'll always be certain things that are part of the sound designer's job though, and these pages have them covered.

All deliberate sound is part of sound design

1) The sound designer is responsible for overseeing everything that makes up the production's overall acoustic style. This includes:
   - Music (live and pre-recorded)
   - Sound effects (live and pre-recorded)
   - Amplification of sound, music and dialogue

A sound designer's mixing desk.

© Mikel Marks / ArenaPAL

2) The sound designer communicates meaning using sound to support the artistic vision of the performance. Sound can be used to communicate time period and location, e.g. a noisy train station.
3) It can also be used to bring out the emotions of a scene and create atmosphere and mood.
4) An audience can be told that a scene is beginning or ending using sound or sudden silences. Sound can also be used during scene changes to keep the performance flowing.
5) Sound designers are responsible for mixing sounds to make sure the whole audience can hear the dialogue clearly. It's important to have the right balance of sounds to avoid distracting the audience.

Some sounds are part of the world of the play...

1) Some sounds can be 'heard' by the characters in the performance (e.g. a doorbell ringing). These are known as diegetic sounds.
2) They might be mentioned in the stage directions or necessary for the plot.
3) Sometimes it's easier if these sounds are pre-recorded. Complex soundscapes (e.g. for a beach scene, crashing waves and seagulls calling) can be played through speakers to create a realistic setting.
4) Some diegetic sounds can be easily produced 'live' in the theatre, like a knock at a door. Noises like shouts, footsteps and animal calls can be made live by offstage actors on cue. These sounds can be timed precisely and often sound more realistic than if they were pre-recorded.
5) Diegetic sounds can communicate dramatic events that take place off stage that might be difficult to show on stage. For example, *Journey's End* takes place in a trench in the First World War — sound effects could be used to create crashes and gunshots to represent trench warfare.

Soundscapes

A soundscape is what's created by layering up sounds to give a strong sense of place. Soundscapes can be made live by actors or pre-recorded.

... and other sounds are outside of it

1) Non-diegetic sounds are sounds which the characters on stage don't 'hear'.
2) Non-diegetic sounds can build atmosphere and tension (e.g. a low rumble might foreshadow a bad event).
3) Music that accompanies a scene but that isn't part of the world of the play is called incidental music. Incidental music can emphasise a particular atmosphere or bring out the emotion in a scene (see p.37).
4) Sound can be symbolic — e.g. in *Macbeth*, a tinkling sound could be used to symbolise that the Witches are mysterious characters. This sound could be played when the Witches enter and at important moments involving the Witches.
5) The frequency and style of this sort of sound varies between productions. Some will have lots of non-diegetic sounds, and others might just use diegetic sounds. The most important thing is that the sound fits in with the overall style of the production.

Sound

Music communicates meaning

1) When incidental music is played quietly during a scene, it's called underscoring.
2) Underscoring might establish a time period or setting (e.g. wartime swing music could transport the audience back to the 1940s), or it might be used to establish an atmosphere.
3) Music can be pre-recorded or played live — a live orchestra can add to the sense of theatrical spectacle. However, this requires more work to make sure that dialogue and sounds are properly balanced.
4) Music can heighten emotion, or set the mood of a scene. It can also contradict the tone of the dialogue, e.g. casual dialogue set over low, foreboding string music might mean something's not right.
5) It's important that any music is used carefully. If it's too noticeable (either because it doesn't fit with the scene or because the volume is wrong) it might be distracting or off-putting for the audience.
6) In musical theatre, songs are an important part of the performance and usually come at key emotional moments. For example, in *Blood Brothers*, the ballad "Tell Me It's Not True" is sung by Mrs Johnstone after she learns her sons have been killed — the emotional climax of the play is heightened by the music.

Equipment can get the best out of the sounds and space

The technical equipment needed for a performance will vary with the style of the show, the size of the theatre and the type of stage. These are some of the things a sound designer could use:

1) Microphones — in some performances, particularly in a large theatre, microphones will be concealed on actors' bodies to pick up their speech and make it audible to the audience. A production with a large cast (e.g. a musical) might use microphones suspended over the stage to pick up groups of voices together.
2) Speakers and amplifiers — amplifiers make sound louder while maintaining its quality, and speakers project sound into the theatre so that everyone can hear. Speaker location affects the audience, e.g. surround sound can make them feel immersed in the action.
3) Mixing desk — this lets the sound designer control the volume of all sounds in relation to each other, so nothing is too loud or quiet when it's heard through the speakers.
4) Software — many sound designers use a computer and cueing software to arrange sounds in the right order so that they can each be played at the press of a button and at the right time.

Sound Levels

Balancing sound levels is crucial. Music and effects need to be heard by the audience without drowning out dialogue. Actors may also need to hear sound cues too.

Sound Check

It's important that all sound equipment is tested before a performance so that the play isn't disrupted by a fault. This is also a chance for the sound levels to be checked and balanced.

A 'cue' is a signal (e.g. a line of dialogue or movement of a character) that tells the lighting and sound technicians when to create an effect.

Make sure you have a sound understanding...

Create a spider diagram of the different sounds used in a production you've seen recently, and explain the effects of the sounds on the audience. Make sure to give examples of the following:

1) Sounds used to give a sense of setting or time period.
2) Incidental music used to add to the atmosphere and emotion of a scene.
3) Sound used to contribute to the play's overall style.

Tick list:
✓ specific sound examples
✓ variety of different types of designed sound
✓ effect on audience

Costume

Costume designers support a play's artistic vision while also trying to keep actors comfortable.

Costumes communicate information

Costume choices can tell the audience a lot about characters and the world of the play:

Time and Place

Costume can signal to an audience when and where action is taking place. For example, actors in shorts and flip-flops would suggest that the play is set somewhere warm.

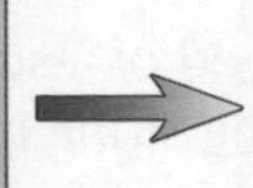

A designer for *An Inspector Calls* could use information from the stage directions and research on early 20th-century middle-class dress to design costumes for the Birlings, e.g. the men would wear dinner suits.

Style

Costumes should fit with the style of the production. A naturalistic play would usually have detailed costumes. An abstract play might use costumes which focus on bringing out a specific mood or symbolic meaning.

In a naturalistic production of *The Crucible*, the characters could wear period dress, but in a minimalist version they might wear plain black clothes, not specific to a time period.

Character and Status

Costume is an efficient way of giving the audience information about characters' backgrounds. It can show differences between characters' wealth, class, age or profession.

A designer for *Blood Brothers* could signal Edward and Mickey's differences in wealth and class by making Edward's clothes cleaner and better fitting than Mickey's.

Colour can emphasise meaning to the audience

1) Colour symbolism is important in costumes (see p.32) — they're a strong visual element of the play.
2) Costume designers can show links or differences between characters, e.g. if all the actors on stage are in black, one wearing white is visually singled out. Colour can also be used to group characters, e.g. in a fight scene, the two sides might each wear a different colour to keep the scene clear for the audience.
3) Costume designers have to think about the colour of the stage lighting. Coloured lights mix with the costume colours and can impact on what the audience sees, e.g. red light turns green costumes grey.

Materials and textures tell the audience about status

1) A high-status character might wear expensive or decorative materials like velvet, silk, lace or gold.
2) The condition of materials is also important for costumes. Coarse wools or cottons might suggest lower status if they're ragged or dirty, but as part of a clean, richly coloured costume they can mean something different.
3) The texture of materials can add to the realism of historical costumes. Real leather or metal can add visual authenticity, and help the audience suspend their disbelief.
4) It's important for designers to think about the practicality of their costumes and how their choice of material will work. Some materials can reduce mobility (e.g. leather or metal), get very sweaty (e.g. PVC) or get hot and itchy (e.g. wool).

Staging

Staging affects how much costume detail an audience can see. With intimate staging, small details of costume and accessories might be visible, so the designer will have to make sure those details are accurate. With a larger stage it's more important that the designer finds ways to give an impression of the costume that the whole audience can see.

Costume

Fit and shape tell an audience about a character

Costume designers make deliberate choices about the fit and shape of clothing to create meaning in ways that the audience can easily see.

1) Clothes can show status and wealth. Poorly fitting clothes might signal lower status and well-fitting clothes might show higher status.
2) It's another way of indicating a character's personality — close-fitting clothes could show that someone is practical and sensible, while baggier clothes might suggest they are more relaxed.
3) Fit is also useful for showing differences between the fashions of different time periods, e.g flared jeans could suggest the 1960s or 70s, and skinny jeans might signal a 2000s setting.
4) The shape of a costume is a key part of characterisation (see p.20), e.g. a bully might have their costume padded out to make their physical presence and character appear more intimidating.
5) Costume designers work closely with the actors and have a strong knowledge of the script. This lets them consider the practicalities of the final performance, including allowing for easy movement on stage and quick costume changes. Actors might also have to be able to make specific or difficult movements, e.g. they might have a fight scene, a dancing scene, or need to move quickly up and down stairs.

In 'An Inspector Calls', the Inspector wears typical detective's clothing to reflect his position and authority.

Stage make-up and hair show age and character

1) Stage make-up and hair are an important aspect of costume design — they're another way of creating a visual impression of a character on stage:

Age
- Making an actor look younger or older is one of the most common uses of stage make-up.
- Young characters' skin might be given a pinkish glow, and older characters might be given wrinkles and grey hair.

Character and Status
- A dirty face and scruffy hair could indicate low status or a carefree nature.
- A mohawk hairstyle might show a rebellious nature, whereas someone more traditional might have a side parting.

Wounds
- Make-up creates specific effects, like realistic wounds and bruises.
- This adds authenticity and can help an audience suspend its disbelief.

Time Passing
- Long stretches of time can be shown by using make-up to age a character between scenes.
- The passing of days and weeks can be shown by changing the characters' hairstyles.

2) Make-up and hair shouldn't seem out of place or distracting — they need to support the overall artistic vision of the performance, and be consistent with the play's style.
3) In a naturalistic play, make-up can add another layer of authenticity. In an abstract style of play, the designer can use make-up to create fantastical effects — e.g. different types of colour, glitter and shadow could be used for the fairies in *A Midsummer Night's Dream* to show they are magical.

Stage make-up — surely that's just wood and nails...

With costume, it's important to remember that everything is deliberate. Think about what the costume tells you about the character's age, status and personality, as well as where and when the play is set.

Masks and Puppets

All sorts of complicated staging problems can be solved by getting masks and puppets involved in the action.

Masks can simplify costume design

1) Masks are common in physical theatre (see p.14). Covering part or all of an actor's face makes voice, movement and staging more important for conveying meaning.
2) Masks can contribute to the overall visual style of the performance. The textures, colours and design of masks will be similar to those used in the sets and costumes.
3) Some masks exist outside the world of the performance — the characters aren't aware they are wearing a mask. This can make it possible to stage things which might be overcomplicated otherwise. They're particularly effective for creating non-human characters on stage, e.g. the farm animals in stage adaptations of *Animal Farm*.
4) When masks exist inside the world of a performance, they are often used to advance the plot, e.g. characters might use them as a disguise.

Romeo and Juliet

In *Romeo and Juliet*, masks are used as a plot device to allow Romeo and his men to sneak into the Capulets' ball without being recognised.

Puppetry is telling stories by moving inanimate objects

1) Puppets are much more common in abstract and physical theatre — they're not often used in naturalistic theatre.
2) Puppetry can add another theatrical dimension to a performance. Puppets are often interesting to look at, and can contribute to the overall visual style of a performance — they might look relatively realistic in colour and size, or they might be more cartoonish and abstract.
3) They're a relatively simple way of staging things that might be too difficult otherwise, e.g. large animals or ghosts.

Puppet design is only an assessment option for AQA — check with your teacher if you're interested in it.

War Horse

In *War Horse*, the horse puppets, designed by the Handspring Puppet Company, are made using wood, rope and leather — materials used in workhorses' equipment. This links to the setting of the play and contributes to the visual style of the performance.

A puppet's physical qualities communicate character

A puppet's facial expression will usually have little or no movement. Designers have to find other ways to add character and depth to puppets:

1) A puppet's size in relation to what it represents and to the stage itself tells the audience about its character. A small puppet might seem vulnerable, whereas a large puppet might seem monstrous. The scale of individual body parts can show meaning too — an unusually large mouth might imply the puppet is talkative or that they like to gossip.
2) A puppet's body shape can tell the audience about its nature, e.g. if its shape is rough and jagged, it might come across as menacing.
3) Colour symbolism is important too (as in all stage design — see p.32).
4) A puppet's materials and texture are a conscious choice made to tell the audience something, e.g. knitted wool or felt may indicate a gentler character, while a welded metal puppet might appear intimidating.

One of the life-sized puppets used in 'War Horse'.

Puppets — the only characters allowed to be wooden...

Not every play is going to have masks and puppets in it, but when they are there, you can be sure it's for a reason. You can read into every little detail of a mask or puppet, so it's worth paying attention to them.

Revision Summary

And that's it for play design. Well, almost — there's just enough space for an exciting revision summary...

- Try these questions and tick off each one when you get it right.
- When you've done all the questions for a topic and are completely happy with it, tick off the topic.

Sets (p.32-33) ☑

1) Give two ways that a set design can create meaning for the audience. ☑
2) Describe three practical concerns a set designer has to think about in their designs. ☑
3) Describe two key features of each of the following:
   a) a naturalistic set
   b) a minimalist set
   c) an abstract set ☑
4) What is a personal prop and how could an actor use one? ☑

Lighting (p.34-35) ☑

5) Give a reason why a lighting designer might want to alter each of the following aspects of lighting:
   a) intensity
   b) colour
   c) direction ☑
6) Name three types of stage lantern and describe how they could be used. ☑
7) What would a lighting designer use to change the colour of a lantern's beam? ☑
8) What is a gobo and how might a lighting designer use one in a performance? ☑

Sound (p.36-37) ☑

9) Describe three roles of sound and music in a production. ☑
10) What is incidental music? ☑
11) What is a soundscape? ☑
12) How might sound be used to suggest time period and location? ☑
13) Name two pieces of sound equipment and describe what they're used for. ☑

Costume (p.38-39) ☑

14) Describe how a costume designer could use a costume to give information about:
    a) time period
    b) location
    c) character ☑
15) Why are a designer's choices of material important in costume design? ☑
16) What practicalities might a costume designer have to think about when creating a design? ☑
17) Describe two ways hair and make-up can be used to create meaning for the audience? ☑

Masks and Puppets (p.40) ☑

18) What role might masks play in a performance? ☑
19) Why might a director choose to use puppets in a performance? ☑

What You Have To Do

That's it with the theory for now. Time to turn your attention to coursework. Up first is the devising element.

Devising involves creating an original performance

1) In the devising part of the course, you have to work as part of a group to create and perform an original piece of theatre based on a stimulus (see p.43) and then evaluate it. Although you'll be working as part of a group, you'll be marked individually.
2) You can choose whether to take the role of a designer or a performer. Both performers and designers should be involved in researching and developing ideas. Once your piece starts to come together, the performers will focus on rehearsals and scripts and the designers will focus on their specific design area.
3) No matter which role you take, you have to complete a portfolio (or devising log). Each exam board has different requirements for the portfolio (see p.54), but it's essentially a record of how you developed and refined your piece, followed by a performance evaluation.

Devising assesses several skills

The devising component is marked on three assessment objectives:

Create and develop ideas to communicate meaning for theatrical performance (**AO1**).

Apply theatrical skills to realise artistic intentions in live performance (**AO2**).

Analyse and evaluate your own work and the work of others (**AO4**).

You need to use your performance and portfolio to prove to the examiner that you:

- can work collaboratively (with other people).
- have a good understanding of style, genre and theatrical conventions (see p.2-18).
- are creative and imaginative.
- can fulfil the aims you set out to achieve when creating your piece (see p.44).
- can evaluate your own work (see p.54-57).
- have developed skills as a performer or designer. This is covered in loads more detail in Sections Two and Three, but in summary, you need to show that you can:

Performance Skills

1) Rehearse and learn lines.
2) Adapt and improve your performance with feedback.
3) Use vocal performance skills.
4) Use physical performance skills.
5) Use characterisation.
6) Communicate with the audience and other performers.

Design Skills

1) Make appropriate judgements during the development process.
2) Create clear and practical designs with thought given to the practical application of materials and production elements.
3) Adjust designs in response to rehearsals.
4) Use design elements to create mood, atmosphere and style.
5) Use design skills during a performance.

The better your teamwork, the better your team's play...

Whether you're a performer or a designer, everyone needs to work together to make sure you produce a top-notch original performance. Don't be that person in the group who isn't pulling their weight.

Devising from a Stimulus

You'll always start your devising piece with a stimulus. So, without further ado...

A stimulus could be almost anything

1) A stimulus is a starting point which should give you some ideas for your devised piece of theatre.
2) It can take different forms — it might be written (like a letter or a poem), it might be visual (like a photo or a sculpture) or it could be something to listen to (like a song or piece of music).
3) The stimulus could be something personal (e.g. a diary entry), or it might be related more broadly to society at a particular time or place (e.g. a news bulletin about an important global event). It could also be something abstract like a word, colour or theme.
4) Your devised piece should show some kind of link back to your original stimulus, but it doesn't have to feature it too closely. It's the way your ideas have developed from the stimulus that's important.
5) Your group will choose from a list of stimuli and then use that choice to develop a performance. Here are some examples:

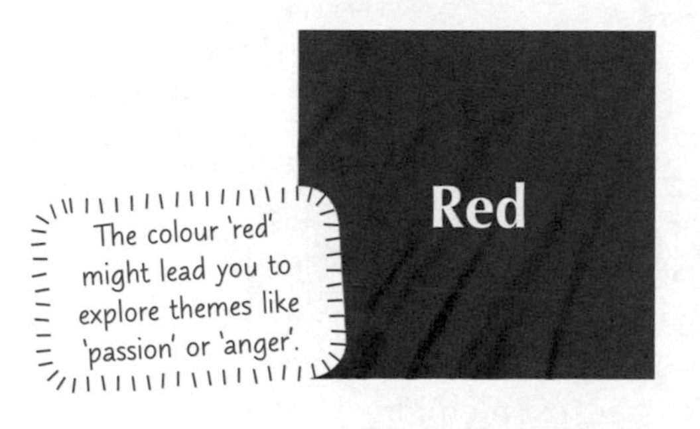

Take care when choosing your stimulus

1) Think about what each stimulus means to you and jot down your first impressions. Then discuss your ideas as a group — there should be lots to think about. Be open to all ideas at this stage.
2) During these initial discussions, think about themes and ideas that are linked to each stimulus, e.g. a photo of a school sports day could suggest themes like childhood and competition.
3) Discuss different options and narrow down your choice. Your chosen stimulus should provide plenty of ideas on themes and topics that you want to explore in more detail.
4) Keep a record of how your group decided on a stimulus — you'll need this for your portfolio.

Group Work

Although you'll be marked individually, this task is all about working together. This means you have to bring together lots of different people's ideas and perspectives. Always try to be a supportive and constructive team member.

Stimulus, stimuli — sounds like a science lesson to me...

Pick one of the three stimuli from this page. Create a spider diagram of all the things it makes you think of. Try to come up with as many ideas as possible, including:

1) Any personal feelings and memories it suggests.
2) Any settings or time periods it suggests.
3) Any themes it suggests.

Tick list:
✓ creating ideas
✓ thinking about a stimulus from different angles

Developing Your Ideas

Now that you've chosen your stimulus, you need to do some research and start developing your piece.

You need to research your chosen stimulus

1) Research is a really important part of devising — it helps you to turn your initial thoughts into developed ideas. If you start writing your piece without researching your stimulus properly, you risk creating something that lacks depth and insight.
2) You can explore your stimulus in different ways. You could do some research using the internet or books, talk to people at home or at school, or watch TV programmes.
3) Think about how best to divide the research between your group — try to play to your individual strengths. Keep a record of all your research and how it helped you to develop your ideas.

Your research will help develop your story

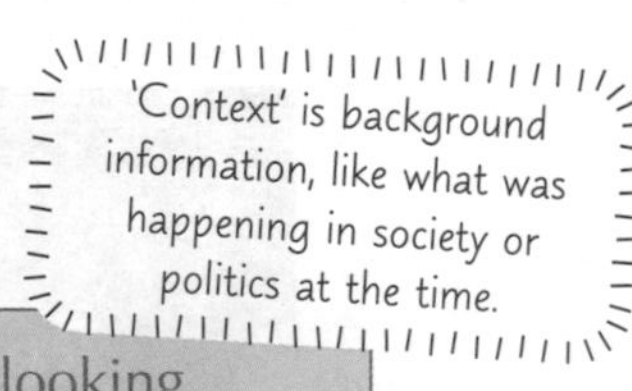

1) Understanding the social, historical and cultural contexts of your stimulus are important. Take a look at this example:

This photograph might just seem like a woman looking unhappy, but if you researched the context you'd discover it's a photograph of a woman called Florence Owens Thompson taken during the Great Depression in America. She worked several jobs, but still struggled to feed her seven children. At the time this photograph was taken, her car had just broken down on the way to find work in a farm. This context could give you some ideas for developing your devised piece.

2) Your research should also involve investigating current themes and trends as well as any issues or controversies from the time your stimulus was created.
3) For example, an article about climate change could lead you to look at websites for environmental charities, where you might find real-life stories to use as inspiration. You could think about how this material could be incorporated into your devised piece to create an emotional or thought-provoking piece of drama.

Decide on the aims and intentions of your piece

1) As you research, you should consider what effect you want to have on your audience.
2) Think about how you want the audience to react to your piece, e.g. with sympathy, admiration, shock, tension or amusement. Thinking about this during the development stage means your characters and scenes will be more focused.
3) Think about whether you want your performance to have an overall message or moral. For example, you may want to challenge the audience's views about something, or persuade the audience to sympathise with certain groups of people.

Dramatic Intentions

It's a good idea to write a Statement of Dramatic Intent — this is an outline of what you want your piece to achieve. This is a requirement for the AQA course, but it's a useful exercise if you're doing another exam board — it'll help your group clarify its main objectives.

Developing Your Ideas

Now it's time to take your stimulus research and develop it further. There are loads of different things you can do to explore your ideas, dialogue and characters — the exercises on this page are definitely worth a try.

Storytelling games help to inspire ideas

1) Storytelling games are a great way of turning your research into ideas.
2) You could play word association games, e.g. if your stimulus is the word 'consequences', you might come up with 'grounded' or 'trouble'.
3) A one-word story is where you each take turns saying a word until a story develops. This can take your ideas in unexpected directions.
4) Creative writing exercises can be really useful too — everyone responds to the stimulus by writing a text, e.g. a fairy tale, diary entry or news story. If any ideas spark the group's imagination, you can then develop them.

© Johan Persson / ArenaPAL

Keep a record of the different exercises you try in your portfolio.

Explore some character development exercises

Once you've got some ideas, you need to create some characters. You can establish your characters' backstory, mood and personality through exercises like:

- Role on the wall — draw the outline of a character on a piece of paper. Inside the outline, write the character's thoughts and feelings. Outside the outline, write down how other people perceive them.
- Hot-seating — an actor answers questions from the group while in character.
- Character questionnaire — write a set of questions that would help to develop a character's depth. Fill one out for each character in your piece.
- Conscience alley — split your group in two and make two lines standing opposite each other. One character walks down the middle and everyone else (either in character or not) gives them advice about a decision the character has to make — this helps the group to understand that character better.
- Park bench — an exercise where characters from your piece meet on a park bench and have to spontaneously interact. This game can develop how your characters talk and act.

For more ideas on how to get into character, see p.23.

Use dramatic techniques to help develop your piece

1) Improvisation is a great way to develop ideas, but it does require some structure. As a group, you'll need to discuss how to approach the improvisation and record all your ideas as you go. For example, you could decide on the first and last line of a scene, and use improvisation to develop the dialogue in the middle.
2) Your group could create a series of tableaux (or freeze frames) in response to the stimulus. This is a great way to generate ideas before adding actions and dialogue.
3) Silence can help you focus on movement and physical theatre. Try acting out a scene without using any dialogue and think about how to create meaning using body language.
4) You could start using design elements — pick a prop or a piece of costume to inspire an improvised scene.

Those exercises read like a list of terrible gameshows...

It's important to explore every aspect of your stimulus and there are plenty of resources and activities that can help you — have group discussions, do plenty of research and use character development exercises.

Developing Your Ideas

Great drama never goes out of style — that's why people are still going on about ol' Billy Shakespeare. Try to pick a style that makes your piece memorable and effective, and works with its genre and form.

Be inspired by companies and practitioners

You can get ideas for developing your piece by looking at how professional companies work together to create effective theatre. Many ideas get discarded long before the performance, but everything they do helps shape its overall vision. Keep a note of all your group's ideas for your portfolio.

For Eduqas, you need to use the techniques of a particular practitioner or the features of a specific genre to inspire your piece.

Frantic Assembly place a lot of importance on collaboration — they listen to each other and try to use everyone's skills effectively.

Think of yourselves as collaborators and decide what everyone brings to the group.

Kneehigh Theatre constantly share and retell their story within the group. They also use a lot of live music and song.

Create a positive atmosphere — share ideas and involve everyone. If one of you is musical, you could use those skills.

The Paper Birds used simple sets and props in their play *In a Thousand Pieces*. The props were re-used in a multi-functional way.

Experiment with simple props or sets and try out different ways of using them.

Odd Doll Puppetry Theatre make use of puppets and live music to create theatre.

You could use some simple puppets to develop and perform your devised piece.

Pick a style for your piece

1) It's important to consider the style of your piece so that you can narrow down the performance techniques you'll use.
2) The style will also influence the set, sound, lighting and costume.
3) Style has an impact on your audience — choose one that's appropriate for your dramatic aims and objectives.
4) Taking inspiration from established theatre makers (like Stanislavski or Brecht, see p.12) will help to influence the style of your own performance. For example:

- Naturalistic drama presents a 'slice of life' on stage. A piece in this style would try to make everything seem as realistic as possible for the audience.
- Epic theatre might be appropriate if your stimulus has an important social or political context. It uses non-naturalistic elements alongside minimal sets and costumes to keep the audience's focus on a message or moral.
- Physical theatre prioritises movement and dance over dialogue. It could work well for a performance based on a musical stimulus, like a song.
- Forum theatre tries to show the audience that they can make a difference to real-life events. A play featuring an injustice is performed twice — on the second run the audience can stop the play and direct the actors to behave differently. It could be appropriate for a piece about a difficult social issue.

See more on theatrical styles on p.12-14.

Steven Berkoff

Berkoff combines movement, music, voice and spectacle to create his drama.

Berkoff's exaggerated physical style used in his 1995 adaption of 'Coriolanus'.

Developing Your Ideas

Think about the genre of your piece

The genre of your piece is closely linked to its style. Genre is important to the overall aims of the performance and the impact you want to have on the audience. It can also help to shape the structure of the piece and offer some ideas for the beginning and ending.

Keep a record of how you made decisions about form, style and genre for your portfolio.

1) If you want to make your audience laugh you could create a comedy (p.7). Look at the different ways of creating comedy, e.g. slapstick, mistaken identity, irony and wit. It could be satirical by poking fun at certain people's attitudes. It could be a parody and make fun of a particular story or style of theatre.
2) If you want your audience to feel shock, pity or sadness you could devise a tragedy. Make sure you include some of its key features, e.g. serious themes and a flawed protagonist (see p.6).
3) You could take a style like documentary or verbatim theatre (p.7) as your inspiration and use the words of real people and real-life stories. This could suit a stimulus based on current affairs.

Form

Think about the form of your devised piece, e.g. a play, musical, mime or mixture of elements from different forms.

Decide how you want to structure your story

Once you've considered genre, style and form, and have some improvised ideas or short scenes, you can start developing your plot. Think about what kind of structure fits your aims best, for example:

- **LINEAR** or **CHRONOLOGICAL** narratives have a beginning, middle and end and everything happens in a real-life time sequence. They're often used in naturalistic performances.
- **CYCLICAL** narratives are non-naturalistic. They often start with a dramatic end scene, then go back to the beginning and gradually build up the tension as the play reaches its ending.
- **EPISODIC** narratives are split into a series of self-contained scenes, which link together but each have their own title and story. These separate episodes can be useful for exploring a particular theme, character or group of characters in a series of different situations.
- **DUAL OR MULTIPLE** narratives tell two or more stories at once, often using techniques like split screen and cross-cutting (see p.18) to show separate storylines. This can be a good way of encouraging your audience to directly compare the events of the two distinct plots.
- **FRACTURED** narratives put scenes in the wrong order, using flashbacks and flashforwards. This keeps the plot ambiguous until the end, creating an atmosphere of confusion and chaos.

Once you have a structure, you can start to create a coherent piece of theatre that fulfils your aims. It will still be rough in places, so the next step is to refine it until it's ready to be performed (see p.48-49).

Devise, don't be divisive — you've got to work together...

Using the stimulus you chose on p.43, come up with three different ideas for the following:

1) A message or moral for your piece.
2) A style for your piece.
3) A genre for your piece.

Tick list:
✓ devising from stimuli
✓ researching and developing ideas
✓ style and genre

Rehearsing and Refining

Practise, polish, perfect, prepare, penguin*, perform — if you remember the six 'P's you'll stay on track to get your devised piece ready on time. Making theatre is as much about planning and timing as the drama itself.

Plan out a rehearsal schedule

Keep your rehearsals focused.

1) Plan your rehearsal schedule backwards from the performance date, leaving at least two weeks at the end for organising the design elements of your piece.
2) During the rehearsal period your devised piece will still be developing, but try to focus on improving what you've got rather than adding new material.
3) If possible, make time to rehearse outside of lessons as well — think of it as practical drama homework.
4) Share different responsibilities between your group, e.g. someone could find the music, another could bring in props, a third could type up a script.
5) It's easier to stay on track if you're organised during each individual rehearsal:

- Decide on an objective for each rehearsal to keep you focused and productive.
- Avoid going over the same section again and again — it could stop you from getting to the end. Block the entire piece first, then go back and polish sections.
- Time your piece regularly and ask your teacher about minimum and maximum performance lengths based on your group's size.

'Blocking' is arranging where actors will stand and how they will move on stage — see p.26 for more.

Don't forget to keep a rehearsal diary for your portfolio

1) Record your progress in a diary — it'll make it easier to remember for your portfolio.
2) Write about how you developed each scene in rehearsal and the techniques you used. Include what worked and what didn't work — you need positive and negative feedback.
3) Note any improvements you made and how you used feedback and editing.
4) Record how your characterisation developed and changed, and the skills you used to do this.

A script can help develop your dialogue

1) Writing a full script is a good way of helping everyone to remember their lines.
2) It can also help develop the structure of your piece by breaking it into scenes and then into dialogue.
3) With a written script, it may also be easier to see which parts of the piece are the most important and if there's anything which can be cut to save on time or edited to make it more effective.
4) You could leave some flexibility in the script to allow for ad-libbing, but it's still good to have some structured dialogue to keep the performance focused.
5) Once you have a script, it's also important to edit and refine the dialogue to make sure the end result sounds as natural as possible.
6) It'll be easier to add stage directions to a written script, which will help performers to remember things like exits, entrances and particular movements. Stage directions are also useful for designers, who might need to plan certain light or sound actions to occur on a certain cue.

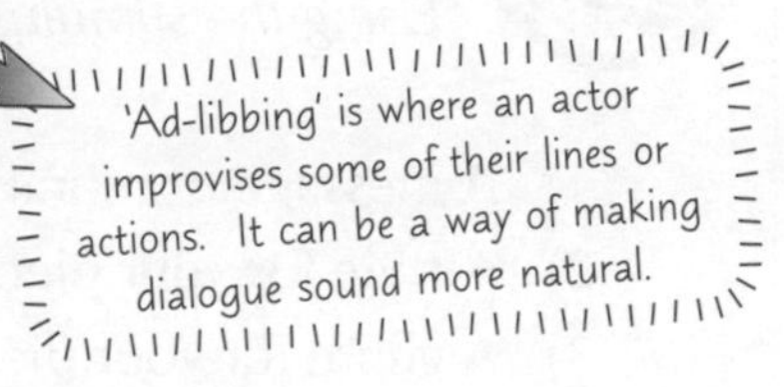

Rehearsing and Refining

Use lesson time to polish and refine your work

You need to improve your performance until it's ready to show to an audience. Here are some ways to do this:

1) Try swapping roles with other group members in key scenes — this will increase your understanding of the character relationships in your piece and make your onstage interactions seem more genuine.
2) Film parts of your rehearsal and watch them back — this is useful for movement sequences to check everyone is in time. It also helps to check you're speaking clearly and using space effectively.
3) Try directing a scene — the members of your group could do a scene each. Use this to check that the dialogue and characterisation are working.
4) If you want to suggest improvements or changes, make sure your feedback is constructive and supportive.

Recording a rehearsal and watching it back can be useful.

Leave enough time to fully prepare for your performance

1) You should have finished your piece at least two weeks before your performance date to give your group enough time to make any final tweaks. If your group doesn't have a designer, this will give you time to think about the costume, sets, lighting and sound.
2) Keep sound and lighting simple, and make sure you write down your cues clearly on cue sheets.
3) Sound effects can help add emotion, atmosphere or a sense of location to the piece — such as spooky music, busy office noises, a car horn or a police siren. Think about how you will create these effects — e.g. using pre-recorded sounds or producing them live.
4) Make sure your costumes are appropriate for the style of your piece — don't just wear your school uniform. Show that you've thought about your character by adding items that identify who you are. If you're playing multiple roles, try to have a 'costume signifier' for each role, e.g. an apron or walking stick.
5) The week before your performance, work on all your transitions (the movements between scenes) and do speed run-throughs where you just focus on your lines. Rehearse with all your props and items of costume, and find time to do a tech rehearsal where you go through all the sound and lighting cues.

Preview Your Devised Piece

- A preview of your devised piece is the last big thing to do before the final performance.
- It'll involve performing your piece to an audience a week before the actual assessment.
- The aim is to get some audience feedback on the piece so you can make some final tweaks.
- It could be really useful to get your audience members to fill in a questionnaire asking them specific questions about their reactions to key moments in the piece and its overall effect.
- As a performer, you should also come away with a sense of how well different parts went. If there was a comic part that didn't get any laughs, or a very serious scene that got loads, think about why the audience reacted differently from what you expected and what changes could fix it.
- The audience feedback and your own feeling of how the performance went should lead you to a final stage of making small adjustments to tighten up your performance before the assessment.

***Ok, so penguin shouldn't be there — it's only five 'P's...**

... but who can blame me? Penguins are great. Devised theatre is also great, particularly if it's planned to perfection. You'll feel a lot better about the performance if you give yourself time to get everything right.

Taking a Design Role

So, you're thinking about taking a design role? Smashing. But before you break out the crayons and the big tub of PVA, there's some important stuff to think about — make sure you understand the way you're assessed.

Design roles have some specific requirements

If you take a design role, you need to consider which element you'll focus on — set, costume, sound or lighting. (Some boards offer puppetry, too.) No matter which you choose, keep the following things in mind:

- It's your designs that are assessed, not your ability to operate equipment.
- There can only be **ONE** designer of each specialism per group.
- You should collaborate with the actors in your group to create your designs.
- Your designs need to be used during the live performance.
- Your notes, sketches and drafts will all need to be seen by the examiner.
- Your designs must be appropriate to the style and content of your piece.
- You must be aware of any health and safety concerns when creating your designs.

Make sure you've got the resources to fulfil your designs

1) Find out early on what facilities your school has for your design area. Knowing what resources are available will make sure your designs are achievable. If your school doesn't have the right equipment, you might have to choose another option instead.
2) If you're a lighting designer, you need to know the different types of stage lantern your school has and how many lighting bars and channels are available.
3) If you're a sound designer, you'll probably need access to microphones, a sound reproduction system and a bank of pre-recorded sounds.
4) Set designers will also need to consider the shape and size of the performance space, and attend rehearsals so that you can see how the performers are using the space.
5) If you're designing costumes or sets, you might have to work within a budget.
6) Costume designers should have access to a range of fabrics.

Approach your design role methodically

There are lots of things you can do to develop and refine your designs:

1) Make a mood board for your design ideas and discuss it with the group to get some feedback.
2) Do some research. You could watch some live theatre, look at images of theatre design and watch instructional videos on how design aspects are created.
3) Make sketches and notes and share these with the group to keep them up-to-date with your ideas.
4) Be flexible — moments in the piece where you'd have used your designs might have to be cut before the final performance. You may also need to adapt your designs as a result of rehearsals, e.g. if a fight scene is added, a costume design might have to be altered to allow for freer movement, or if a scene's time of day is changed, you might have to adapt your lighting design.
5) Keep looking back at your dramatic intentions to make sure your designs effectively communicate your message to the audience.

The Devising Process

During rehearsals, contribute as much as possible to the devising process — designers are just as important as the actors. Make sure to record all your input, ideas and decisions in your portfolio.

Taking a Design Role

You could design the lighting...

1) As a lighting designer, you'll create one lighting design for the final performance.
2) Your design should use a range of different types of lantern — find creative ways of establishing mood and atmosphere to show a range of effects and techniques (see p.35).
3) You also need to provide the sketches, cue sheets and lighting plot to explain your design ideas.
4) You need to supervise the rigging, plotting and focusing of the lights, but for most exam boards you don't have to operate them yourself. For OCR you do need to operate the lighting board during the performance (though you're still not marked on your ability to operate the equipment).

A lighting plot is a detailed plan showing how each lantern should be hung, focused and coloured.

... or the sound...

- If you choose to be a sound designer, you'll create a sound design for the final performance.
- You should use a range of different sounds and transitions in your design — vary things like how sounds stop and start, sound duration and intensity. They could be made live or pre-recorded, depending on how easy a given sound is for an offstage performer to reproduce (see p.36).
- Create source sheets explaining where you got your sound effects and a detailed cue sheet mapping out when each sound will be played, for how long and at what volume.
- Consider the effects your sounds will create for the audience, e.g. tension or a sense of location.
- For OCR, you'll need to work the sound board in the performance (though that won't be marked.)

... or the costumes...

1) As a costume designer, you'll make costumes for either one or two actors (depending on exam board).
2) Create sketches, labelled designs and a costume plot for your designs. A costume plot is a list of all items of costume and any changes that happen during the performance.
3) Your design can include hair, wigs, make-up and masks, and must be worn by a character in the performance. Consider how your design reflects things like age, personality and status.
4) Think about practicalities — the materials you use and the fit of the costume should allow the performer to move freely (see p.52).
5) You should supervise the making or buying of the costume (though you're not assessed on this).

Costumes should suit the genre and style of the production.

... or the set

1) As a set designer, you'll create a complete design for one setting including set dressing and props.
2) You need to produce a final drawing of your design, plus ground plans (the layout of the stage from above), sketches and notes. Some boards require a scale model of your design (check with your teacher).
3) You need to supervise the construction or hiring of the set, but you don't have to do it yourself.
4) You should use shapes, textures and colours to create meaning and suit the content of the devised piece, e.g. in a naturalistic piece the set should be realistic and believable.

Puppet Design

AQA offers the option to design a puppet for the performance. You'll need to provide designs and sketches for the puppet used. You'll be marked on the design itself, not on its construction or operation.

Taking a Design Role

Your design should convey mood, atmosphere and style

Whichever aspect of design you choose, you'll need to work with the actors and other designers to make sure that your piece is clear and consistent.

- CONTEXT — Make sure your designs suit the play's context and accurately reflect the play's setting. For example, if your performance is set in the 1800s, you could try to replicate candlelight using electric candles, or source the sound of horse-drawn carriages.
- STYLE — Make sure you're aware of the conventions of your piece's style. For example, a piece of Epic Theatre would be non-naturalistic, so the set, costumes, lighting and sound would be simple.
- GENRE — If your group has devised a comedy, you could use bright costumes, lighting and sets to add to the light-hearted mood of the piece. You might use upbeat music and over-the-top sound effects too. If your group is producing a tragedy, sombre colours, lighting and sounds would be more appropriate.
- DRAMATIC AIMS — If your piece has a message, your designs can reinforce it. For example, you may decide to dress a character who faces injustice differently from the other actors to highlight how they feel separated from society.
- ATMOSPHERE — The atmosphere of a piece may change, so this is a good opportunity to show your versatility as a designer. If you want to create tension, you could use sound effects to mimic a human heart beating quickly. The heartbeat could slow and fade out as the tension decreases.

Consider practicalities in your designs

You also need to consider the more practical aspects of your chosen design area:

1) During rehearsals, keep track of what requirements the performers have to be able to play their parts effectively, e.g. their costumes might need to allow them to perform certain movements.
2) Also think about what the plot of your piece needs in relation to your design area — there might need to be a certain sound, or the time of day might change. If you're designing the set, make sure you provide enough entrances and exits, and position them to make the best use of the space.
3) Be sensible with the techniques or materials you use to fulfil your designs. For example, if you're a set designer, don't use unnecessarily heavy materials or complicated sets if there's a simpler solution. If you're a sound designer, there's not much point in going to the effort of recording someone knocking on a door if this could easily be made live on the day.
4) It's also really important to consider any possible health and safety issues in your design (see p.53).

It's everyone's responsibility to think about health and safety.

REVISION TASK

Lost? Confused? Just read de-signs...

Choose a scene from a play you're studying. Create an annotated design sketch for this scene in your chosen specialism. Make sure you answer all of the following questions:

1) What do you want your designs to signify to the audience?
2) How are they linked to your dramatic intentions?
3) How do your designs fit with the style of your piece?

Tick list:
✓ approaching design
✓ design specialisms
✓ style and dramatic intentions

Health and Safety

Right, serious hats on now, everyone. We'll have none of that "healthy and safety gone mad" nonsense here. This is an incredibly important part of theatre for everyone involved, and designers have a crucial role to play.

Stay safe around electrical equipment

1) Electrical equipment is a high risk part of theatre design, so extra care is needed when using it.
2) Don't bring in any equipment of your own without asking your teacher first. All electrical equipment needs to be safety tested by someone with training.
3) It's dangerous to work with electrical equipment while it's 'live', so make sure lanterns are switched off and disconnected before changing their angle or adding gobos and gels.
4) Check that cables and wires are tied down securely and out of the way of areas people will be walking so that they're not a trip hazard.

Be aware of safety issues with costumes and make-up

1) Make sure the performers are aware if a costume has any pins in it when they're trying it on.
2) Some performers may be allergic to certain fabrics — always check with them first, and allow time for the costume to be tried on and altered if the issue does arise.
3) When designing make-up, always conduct a patch test on the performers — this involves trying a small amount of make-up on the actor's skin to test for allergies.
4) When applying make-up, always use clean make-up applicators, and don't use the same brushes or sponges on more than one person. This is to prevent infection and contamination.

Safety For Performers

Performers need to take care too. Be careful not to fall if your set uses raised levels or rostra, or if you're near the stage edge. Also be careful if you're doing any 'action scenes'. Don't injure yourself or others when carrying out physical movements.

There are many potential hazards in a theatre

1) You shouldn't work at height (up ladders or scaffolding) unless you're trained.
2) Anyone lifting heavy equipment should bend at the knees to prevent back strain. Protective shoes and gloves should be worn for these jobs.
3) Falling objects are a risk when someone is working up a ladder. If you are supervising the installation of lights, ensure the space is clear and don't stand directly below the ladder.
4) There are also some things you should always do before a performance:

- Check that all aisles, backstage areas and staging are free from trip hazards.
- Check that the fire exits are not blocked by any of your equipment.
- If you have installed staging or rostra, check that it's all bolted together securely.
- If you are planning to use any loud noises or strobe lighting effects, you should notify the audience before the production starts to make sure they don't trigger any health issues.

Sorry folks, but health and safety is no joke...

... so there'll be no wisecracks from me this time. You need to do everything you can to prevent anyone getting hurt during rehearsals or performance (including yourself). If you're ever unsure, just ask for help.

Portfolio

The performance is only part of the devising assessment — you also need to put together a cracking portfolio. It's important to work on your portfolio alongside your devised piece — don't leave it until the last minute.

Your portfolio is a record of the devising process

1) You'll produce a portfolio or log of your ideas to accompany your devised performance or design.
2) Different sections of your portfolio will be about the different stages of devising, from your initial ideas and how you developed them, through to an evaluation of your performance or design.
3) You should begin gathering material and making notes for your portfolio as soon as you are given your stimuli. You'll keep working on it alongside the devising process.
4) The length and structure of your portfolio will vary depending on your exam board. Make sure you check what you need to do with your teacher.
5) The format of your portfolio differs between exam boards, but generally you can present it as a piece of written work (of 1500-2500 words), or an image-based, audio or video portfolio (you could also use a combination of these formats — check the details with your teacher).

Different exam boards have different requirements

The exam boards differ in how they want you to approach and structure your portfolio. Some of the differences are minor, but some are important, so it's worth knowing what your own exam board wants.

AQA

The AQA portfolio is called the 'devising log' and is made up of three elements:

- The first is a record of your initial response to your chosen stimulus.
- The second is about the process of collaborating to develop your piece.
- The third consists of the analysis and evaluation of the devising process and your final performance.

Eduqas

The Eduqas portfolio has three elements:

- The first is about how your ideas were researched, created and developed.
- You need to incorporate the style of a particular practitioner or genre for Eduqas — the second section is an explanation of how you went about doing this.
- The third part is about how your ideas were developed, edited and refined.
- Each element must include some illustrative material, e.g. photos or annotated diagrams.

For Eduqas, remember that you complete your performance evaluation separately from the portfolio and under timed conditions.

Edexcel

The Edexcel portfolio has six elements:

- The first is about your initial response to your stimulus and your dramatic intentions.
- The second is about your group's process of exploring your chosen stimulus.
- The third records the development process, including any significant moments or turning points that occurred.
- The fourth section is about how you used genre, structure, character, form, style and language.
- The fifth is a discussion about how effective your contribution to the performance was.
- The sixth is an evaluation of how successful you were in achieving your dramatic aims.

OCR

The OCR portfolio has three elements:

- The first is about your initial ideas and how you researched your chosen stimulus.
- The second is about how you created and developed the original material of your piece (this should include analysis and evaluation of your work in progress).
- The third is an analysis and evaluation of the final performance and the devising process.

Portfolio

Here are some examples of how you might approach different sections of your portfolio.

Describe your initial response to your chosen stimulus

1) Explain your personal thoughts in response to the stimuli you were offered and the process you went through to choose a stimulus. It's important to refer to your own contribution to these group decisions.
2) This example paragraph about a student's initial response is good — it explains the decision and gives specific examples. It gives evidence of the student's personal contribution, but it also shows that the group worked collaboratively.

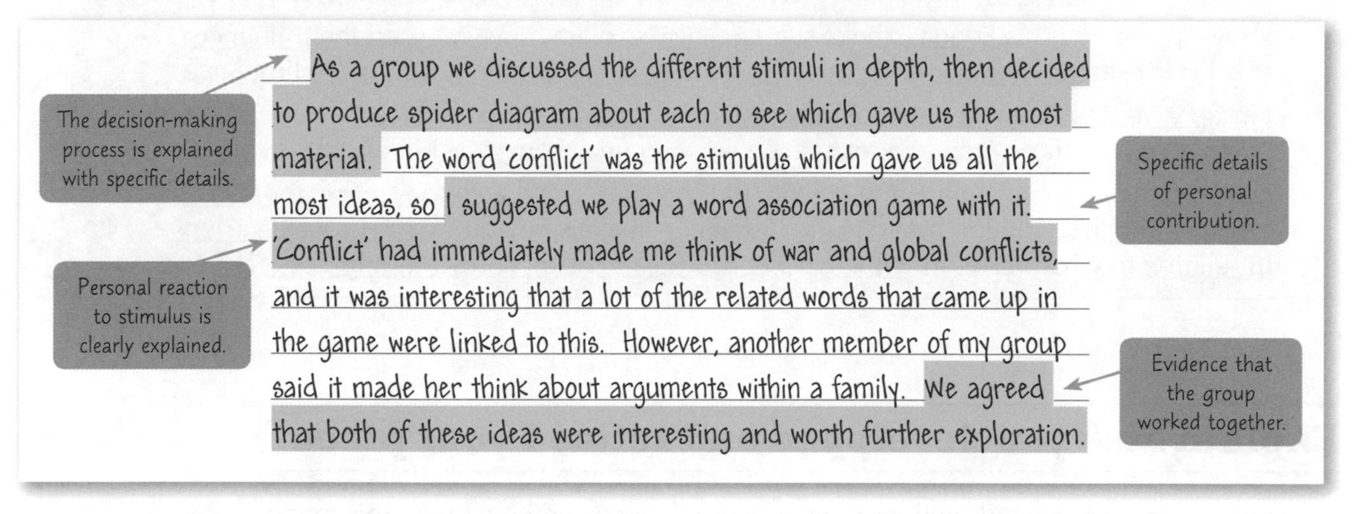

Then explain how you researched your stimulus

1) Note down the methods you used to research your stimulus, and how your research helped to develop your ideas.
2) When writing about your research, try to be specific. Include quotes from your research, as well as any relevant pictures, facts and figures.
3) Record what your dramatic aims are at this point. You might end up describing how they change during the devising process, but it's good to show you have some clear aims early on.
4) Have a look at this example of a successful explanation of the research stage:

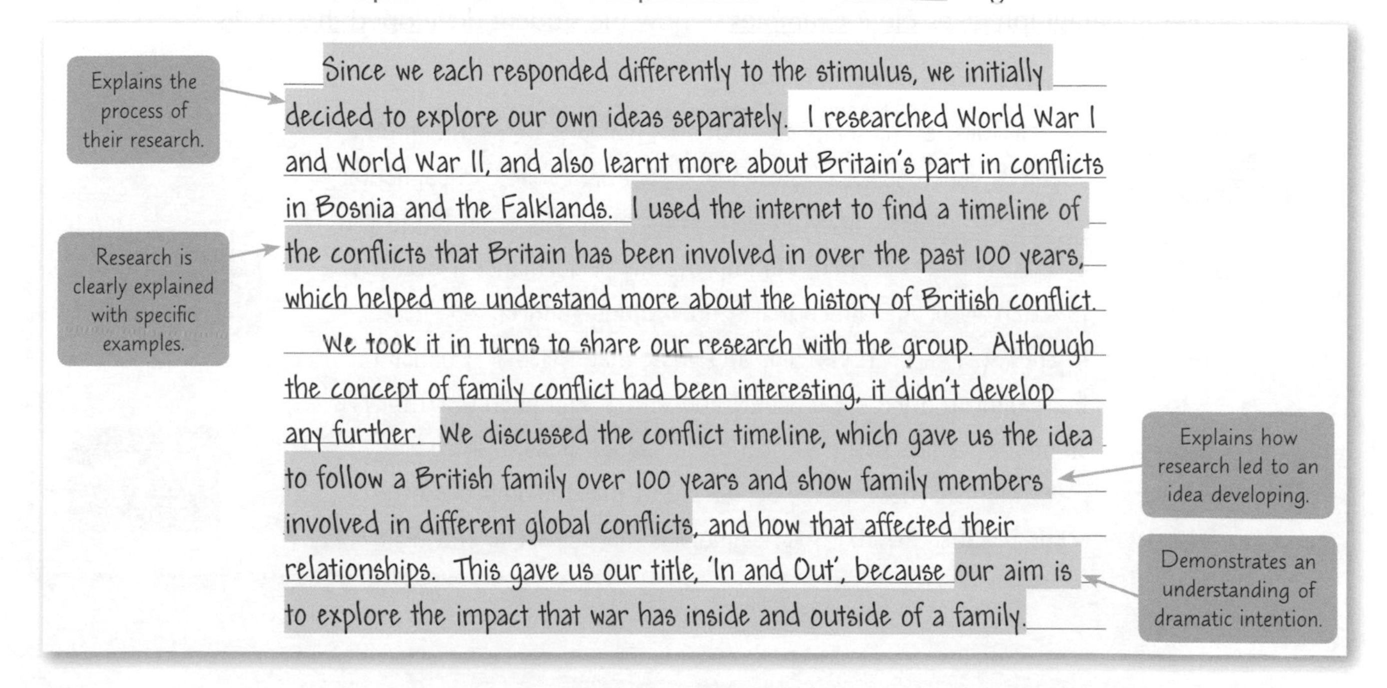

Portfolio

Write about the ways you generated original material

Next, you need to explain how you turned your ideas and research into a piece of drama.

- Give details of the practical methods you used to create the plot, characters and dialogue, e.g. group improvisation, storytelling games or hot-seating (see p.23 for more suggestions).
- Explain which methods were useful and which weren't, and why you think this might have been.
- Talk about how you used genre, style, form and structure to create material, e.g. deciding to develop your piece as a tragedy might have given you some strong ideas about how the plot could end.
- If your exam board is Eduqas, make sure you also explain how you used the influence of your chosen practitioner or theatrical style to generate material from your stimulus.
- Group work is a really key part of the creation of material. Make it clear in your portfolio how you worked as a team to generate drama, using specific examples.
- When explaining how you came up with the material, you'll get more marks for showing a strong understanding of how theatre is made — make sure you explain your decisions in relation to what makes an effective piece of theatre using correct terminology.

Explain how you developed and refined your piece

1) Explain how you refined sections of your devised piece and how doing this made the piece flow better as a whole — make sure you include specific examples.
2) Be aware of any significant moments in your devised piece — any points that are key for the plot, character development or emotional arc of the piece. Pay particular attention to these when explaining how you went about refining and developing your performance.
3) Describe how you applied your own skills (not just the improvements you decided on together as a group) and explain how you developed and refined your characterisation using examples.
4) If you're a designer, give specific examples of how your skills improved throughout the process.
5) Make a note of any feedback you receive from your teacher or from members of your group, and explain how you used it to improve your own performance and refine the piece as a whole.
6) The following paragraph gives clear examples of how the student developed their skills.

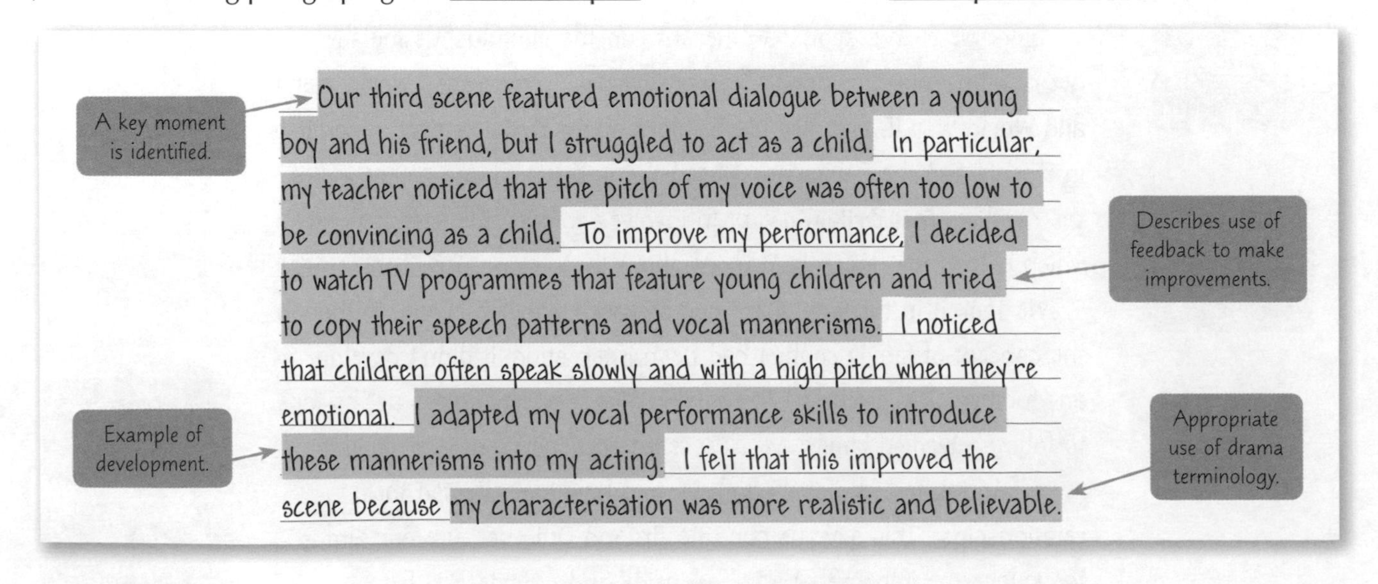

Portfolio

After your performance you need to analyse it...

ANALYSING is exploring the impact your creative decisions and performance had on the audience.

1) Think about your contribution to the final performance and describe the impact it had on the audience.
2) Pick out key moments from the performance, and explain the specific performance or design skills you used that made them effective.
3) Make sure you use the correct dramatic terminology.
4) This example analyses the performance using clear explanations and specific examples.

Describes the dramatic intention.

Appropriate terminology is used.

My character, Matthew, had been bullied because his mum died in conflict. My aims were to show how much Matthew had been changed by bullying, and to create sympathy for him from the audience. Throughout the piece, I gradually altered my posture from a confident, upright stance to a more hunched, withdrawn posture, and stopped smiling or using eye contact. I also used pauses and stuttering in my final monologue to show how broken Matthew had become. I believe these techniques had the effect of creating sympathy for him.

Specific examples of dramatic skills are given.

Analyses the effect on the audience.

... and evaluate how well it went

EVALUATING is examining what did or didn't go well, the reasons why and what you'd do differently.

1) Judge how successful your own contribution to the piece was. Think about what went well or didn't go so well, and give specific examples.
2) Think about the piece as a whole as well. Discuss whether it achieved your dramatic aims and give reasons why or why not.
3) Consider the things you would do differently next time. For example, you might mention developing a particular skill more fully, or editing your piece differently.

Focuses on the impact on the audience.

Discusses a specific moment which could be improved.

Although I feel my use of performance skills was generally successful in creating sympathy for my character and showing the effects of bullying, there were certain things I could have done differently. For instance, I think the final moments of the play after my monologue would have been more moving if, instead of loudly breaking down in tears, I had used silence and stillness and was more reserved. This would have made Matthew seem much more withdrawn and defeated by the bullying than my original choices did.

Examples of which skills were used and what changes could be made.

Thinks about the effect the changes would have.

Portfolio, portfolio, wherefore art thou portfolio...

Your portfolio isn't the sort of thing you can do at the last minute — you'll need to be organised and plan it properly from the beginning. You don't want to ruin a great devised piece with a rushed portfolio.

Performing From a Text

It's worth knowing what you need to do in the performance component of GCSE Drama. You don't want to get the wrong idea and be the only person doing a three hour, postmodern jazz rendition of Humpty Dumpty.

Start by studying the play as a whole

1) In this part of GCSE Drama, you'll perform or make designs for some play extracts. You'll be expected to:

   *Apply theatrical skills to realise artistic intentions in live performance (**AO2**).*

   For OCR, you'll also be assessed on AO1.

2) This means you should be able to show how your performance or design creates meaning, achieves your artistic intentions and shows a wide range of performance or design skills.
3) You'll study the whole play first to give you an understanding of the genre, style, structure, language and themes of the play. It will also give you a better sense of characters' motivations, and you'll develop an overall sense of the playwright's intentions and the play's context.
4) You'll then interpret and rehearse two key extracts from the play. These extracts could be monologues, duologues or group scenes (check with your teacher what you need to do).
5) You can choose to take the role of a performer or a designer — if you're a designer you'll choose an aspect of design to work with, e.g. lighting, costume or sets.
6) You'll prepare and put on a performance of your extracts for a live audience and an examiner.

You need to make your artistic intentions clear

1) You also need to write a Statement of Artistic Intention — this is a brief written record of what you set out to achieve through your performance or design.
2) It should explain the theatrical choices you've made in your performance or design. It isn't marked (except for OCR), but the examiner will use it to mark your performance.

   It's worth quite a few marks with OCR — ask your teacher.

3) It's also important to have thought about the playwright's intentions and how your performance communicates your interpretation of these intentions. Here are some of the things you need to cover:

Performers — talk about how you've interpreted your character. Explain things like the feelings and motivations of your character and how you plan to show them through your movement and vocal techniques. Discuss the effect you want to have on the audience.

Designers — talk about how you've interpreted the scenes. Explain how you've used the text to inform your designs and how you've created meaning using specific techniques.

Designers should be as involved as the performers in the creative process from the start.

An examiner will watch your performance

1) A visiting examiner will use your Statement of Artistic Intention to assess how well you've achieved what you set out to do. They'll watch your live performance and award marks based on how you do.
2) As a performer, you'll be marked on your own individual performance. The examiner will watch for how you use vocal techniques and physicality to effectively characterise your role and communicate your intentions to the audience.
3) As a designer, you'll need to check with your teacher about how you'll be marked. For most exam boards, you're only marked on the designs themselves, rather than actually making or controlling them.

A performance of 'DNA'.

Performing From a Text

Rehearsals are a chance for you to get to grips with your text and add your own spin to your performance.

You could take the role of a performer or a designer

1) Your teacher will make sure your chosen extracts give everyone in your group a chance to show a range of performing or designing skills (and take the right length of time to perform).
2) You can perform a lead or supporting role — this won't affect how many marks are available for your performance. The key thing is to make sure you're showing off specific performance skills.
3) You might decide to take on the role of a designer instead — you could be in charge of the lighting, sound, set or costumes. The same amount of marks are available for each.
4) Find ways to develop your own interpretation of the extracts. If you're performing, there are lots of techniques you can use to explore your character (e.g. hot-seating, thought-tracking and role on the wall — see p.45). If you're designing, you could research the period that the play is set in to ensure that the scenery, props, hair and make-up are authentic.

You'll need to understand the play's genre, form and structure to be able to put your extract in context.

Rehearsal and preparation are key to success

1) You'll need to organise your rehearsal schedule between your group. Make sure you leave plenty of time to practise everything. Use your rehearsals to develop your ideas and refine your performance.
2) You may need to do several different types of rehearsals to allow everyone in your group to practise their roles.
3) A dress rehearsal will allow you to try out any props or costumes you'll use during the performance. Getting used to them will help you to work them naturally into your performance and reduce the chance of anything going wrong on the day.
4) A technical rehearsal should concentrate on things like the lighting, sound and scenery to make sure everything is set up correctly so there are no surprises on performance day.
5) During rehearsals, make sure you think about proxemics, blocking and sightlines. On assessment day, you might give the performance of your life, but if the examiner can't see you properly, you might not get the marks you deserve.
6) On the day of your performance, you'll probably feel nervous. Remember that the audience are on your side, and find ways to help yourself focus on what you have to do. Warming up your body and voice can be a really good way of getting yourself in the right frame of mind.
7) Most performances go smoothly, but sometimes things don't go to plan — a prop might not work, or an actor might forget a line. The best thing to do in these situations is to carry on in character.

Tips for Learning Lines

- Read aloud — get used to how your lines feel and sound when you say them.
- Move about — practising them while walking around or doing your actions from the scene can help lines stick in your head. Muscle memory will help you retain them.
- Practise with someone — ask someone to read the other characters' lines. This will help you learn the cues that lead up to your lines.
- Highlight your lines — marking out your own lines on the page can help your visual memory.

You should know your lines like the back of your hand...

... so that you don't have to actually write them on the back of your hand. Preparation for your performance is important — plenty of rehearsals should ensure that there are no surprises on the day.

Performance Skills

Here's how you might take an extract from page to stage

This extract is from Act 2, Scene 2 of *Macbeth*. Macbeth has gone to murder King Duncan, and Lady Macbeth is waiting for him to return. The annotations suggest how you might use physical and vocal skills to perform the role of Lady Macbeth.

Remember: you need to perform two extracts. Think about how your character changes and develops.

COURTYARD IN MACBETH'S CASTLE

Enter LADY MACBETH

LADY MACBETH That which hath made them drunk hath made me bold;
What hath quenched them hath given me fire. Hark! Peace!
It was the owl that shrieked, the fatal bellman,
Which gives the stern'st good-night. He is about it.
The doors are open, and the surfeited grooms
Do mock their charge with snores — I have drugged their possets,
That death and nature do contend about them,
Whether they live or die.

MACBETH *(Within)* Who's there? What, ho!

LADY MACBETH Alack, I am afraid they have awaked,
And 'tis not done. The attempt and not the deed
Confounds us. Hark! I laid their daggers ready;
He could not miss 'em. Had he not resembled
My father as he slept, I had done't.

Enter MACBETH

My husband!

MACBETH I have done the deed. Didst thou not hear a noise?

LADY MACBETH I heard the owl scream and the crickets cry.
Did not you speak?

MACBETH When?

LADY MACBETH Now.

MACBETH As I descended?

LADY MACBETH Ay.

MACBETH Hark!
Who lies i' the second chamber?

LADY MACBETH Donalbain.

MACBETH (*Looking at his hands*) This is a sorry sight.

LADY MACBETH A foolish thought, to say a sorry sight.

MACBETH There's one did laugh in's sleep, and one cried 'Murder!'
That they did wake each other — I stood and heard them,
But they did say their prayers, and addressed them
Again to sleep.

LADY MACBETH There are two lodged together.

MACBETH One cried 'God bless us!' and 'Amen' the other,
As they had seen me with these hangman's hands.
List'ning their fear, I could not say 'Amen'
When they did say 'God bless us.'

LADY MACBETH Consider it not so deeply.

MACBETH But wherefore could not I pronounce 'Amen'?
I had most need of blessing and 'Amen'
Stuck in my throat.

LADY MACBETH These deeds must not be thought
After these ways; so, it will make us mad.

Lady Macbeth's monologue shows her agitation. You could pace around the stage to reflect this.

Lady Macbeth thinks that she can hear something. You could include a pause after "Hark!" to show that she is listening carefully.

Lady Macbeth is paranoid. These lines could be said with a fast pace to reflect her inner turmoil.

Lady Macbeth says that she would have killed Duncan herself if he hadn't reminded her of her father. This shows a more human side to Lady Macbeth, so you could perform this quietly with a softer tone.

Lady Macbeth is relieved that Macbeth has returned. This line could be performed with an excited tone. You could go to Macbeth and embrace him to show your relief.

These short lines could be spoken with a quick pace to show Lady Macbeth's agitation and to increase the tension.

Lady Macbeth doesn't say much in these lines, but think about how you would use active listening to react to Macbeth's dialogue. You could cover your mouth to show shock or lean forward to show that you are listening carefully.

Lady Macbeth wants Macbeth to calm down. You could take hold of him by the shoulders to show that you are being stern with him.

This line foreshadows Lady Macbeth's madness later in the play. These lines could be spoken slowly to emphasise their importance.

Design Skills

You could design the settings and props...

You might decide to design another aspect of the extracts, for example sound or puppetry.

This extract is from Act 4, Scene 1 of *Macbeth*. The Witches are creating a potion.

A DESERTED PLACE NEAR FORRES
Thunder. Enter the three WITCHES.

FIRST WITCH — Thrice the brindled cat hath mewed.
SECOND WITCH — Thrice and once the hedge-pig whined.
THIRD WITCH — Harpier cries, "'Tis time, 'tis time."
FIRST WITCH — Round about the cauldron go,
In the poisoned entrails throw.

You could use a cyclorama to show a forest background swaying in the stormy weather.

A smoke machine could create fog which would add to the mysterious atmosphere.

Knotted rope could be used to represent entrails. An actor could store the rope in their pockets and then throw it in the cauldron.

The dialogue mentions a cauldron, so you could position one in the centre of the stage. You could use coloured fairy lights beneath it to mimic a fire, and a smoke machine inside the cauldron could release jets of steam.

... the costume, hair and make-up...

This extract is from Act 5, Scene 1 of *Macbeth*. Lady Macbeth is sleepwalking and has gone mad from guilt.

Lady Macbeth is sleepwalking, so she could wear a nightdress to demonstrate this to the audience. You could research what a noblewoman's nightdress from the medieval period would look like to make it look as authentic as possible.

Even though Lady Macbeth is washing imaginary blood from her hands, you could stain the actor's hands red to make the audience question what is real and what is an illusion.

LADY MACBETH — Out, damned spot! Out, I say! One, two: why, then, 'tis time to do't. Hell is murky! Fie, my lord, fie! A soldier, and afeard? What need we fear who knows it, when none can call our power to account? Yet who would have thought the old man to have had so much blood in him?

You could use face powder to make the actor playing Lady Macbeth look pale. This would highlight her guilt and anxiety.

Lady Macbeth is agitated and distressed. Her hair could be knotted and tangled to suggest that she has been tossing and turning in her sleep.

... or the lighting

These are just a few examples of how you could design different aspects of an extract. Your versions should contain more detail, and the extracts you use will be longer.

This extract is from Act 1, Scene 3 of *Macbeth*.
Banquo and Macbeth meet the Witches for the first time.

Enter MACBETH *and* BANQUO.

MACBETH — So foul and fair a day I have not seen.
BANQUO — How far is't called to Forres? What are these,
So withered and so wild in their attire,
That look not like th'inhabitants o'th'earth,
And yet are on't? Live you, or are you aught
That man may question? You seem to understand me,
By each at once her choppy finger laying
Upon her skinny lips; you should be women,
And yet your beards forbid me to interpret
That you are so.
MACBETH — Speak if you can: what are you?
FIRST WITCH — All hail Macbeth! Hail to thee, Thane of Glamis!
SECOND WITCH — All hail Macbeth! Hail to thee, Thane of Cawdor!
THIRD WITCH — All hail Macbeth that shalt be king hereafter!

At first, the Witches could be lit by a dim profile spotlight, which could get brighter when Banquo notices them.

Dim lighting on stage would create a menacing atmosphere. You could also use a blue gel over the lights to make the scene feel cold and eerie.

You could use gobos to create a dappled effect. The shadows would create a mysterious atmosphere.

You could use a harsh spotlight to illuminate each of the Witches when they speak. Using the spotlight would draw the audience's attention to the actors and suggest what they are saying is important.

Set Text Question

This is it — the big moment you've been waiting for (or dreading). Unfortunately, you can't get out of doing the written exam. What you can do is make it easier for yourself by learning what to expect on the day.

The exam will ask a range of questions

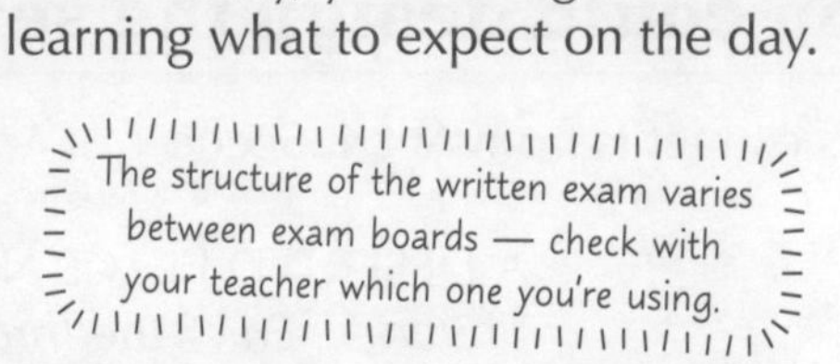
The structure of the written exam varies between exam boards — check with your teacher which one you're using.

1) In the written exam, you'll be expected to:

Demonstrate knowledge and understanding of how drama is developed and performed (**AO3**).

2) In order to demonstrate this skill, you'll need to answer questions on a set play that you've studied. These questions might focus on an extract from the play...

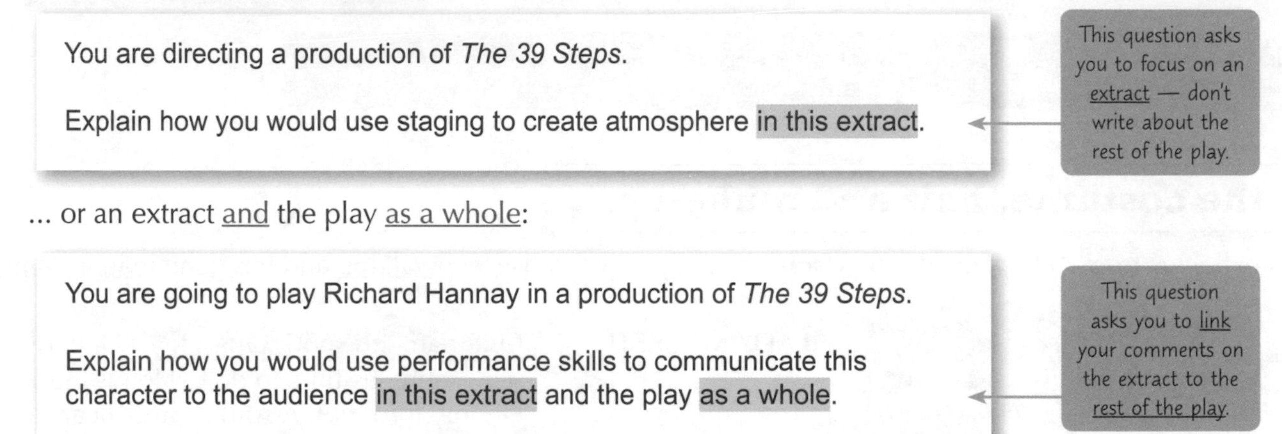
You are directing a production of *The 39 Steps*.

Explain how you would use staging to create atmosphere in this extract.

This question asks you to focus on an extract — don't write about the rest of the play.

... or an extract and the play as a whole:

You are going to play Richard Hannay in a production of *The 39 Steps*.

Explain how you would use performance skills to communicate this character to the audience in this extract and the play as a whole.

This question asks you to link your comments on the extract to the rest of the play.

3) Some questions use bullet points to tell you what to write about:

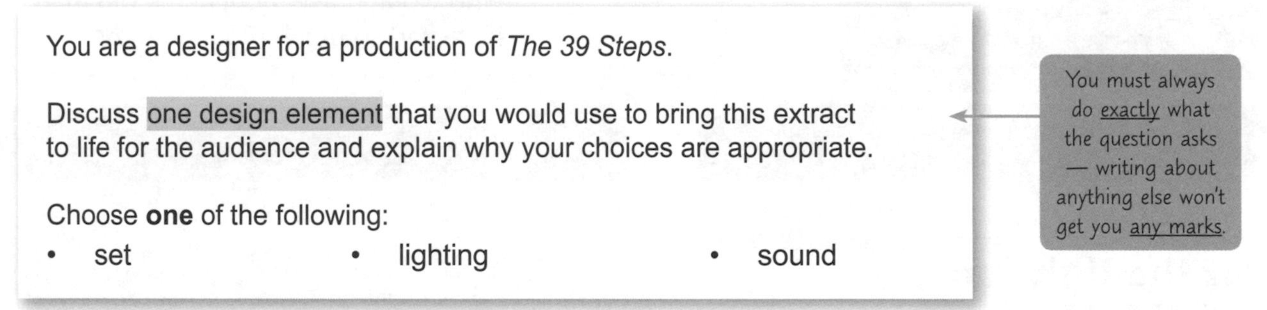
You are a designer for a production of *The 39 Steps*.

Discuss one design element that you would use to bring this extract to life for the audience and explain why your choices are appropriate.

Choose **one** of the following:
- set
- lighting
- sound

You must always do exactly what the question asks — writing about anything else won't get you any marks.

4) Some exam boards use shorter questions to build up to the longer questions — they might ask about theatre roles and terminology or they might ask about a play you've studied. If this applies to you, you'll need to check the number of marks available for each question so you can manage your time effectively.

You'll answer from different perspectives

1) As shown above, you can be asked to write from the perspective of a performer, designer or director:

- As a **PERFORMER**, you'll need to think about how you would use your performance skills to portray a certain character. This includes a combination of physical skills and vocal skills.
- As a **DESIGNER**, you'll need to come up with design ideas that would enhance the impact of the play. This requires a good understanding of design elements like set, lighting and sound.
- As a **DIRECTOR**, you'll need to consider how you would bring the written text to life on stage. You'll be asked to focus on one element of the production, rather than the play as a whole.

2) You can't just learn about the roles and responsibilities of one type of theatre maker — over the course of the written exam, you might be expected to answer from all three perspectives.

Set Text Question

Think about the different aspects of the text

No matter whose perspective you're writing from, there are some general points you'll need to consider:

Playwright's Intentions

Think about what the playwright is trying to achieve and how this could be interpreted. Make sure you look at and consider the stage directions.

Context

Identify any aspects of the historical, social and cultural context (see p.4) that might have an effect on the way it's performed, designed or directed.

© Johan Persson / ArenaPAL

Roles of Theatre Makers

Develop an understanding of the roles and responsibilities of theatre makers (see p.3) in bringing the text to life, as well as any challenges they might face.

Characteristics of Texts

Pick out important details about the text (e.g. style, genre and structure), and consider the ways these might be communicated to the audience.

All good answers have some things in common...

If you want to achieve top marks in the written exam, your answers should always include the following:

- TECHNICAL LANGUAGE — use accurate terminology to describe each aspect of a production, such as performance skills, design features and stage configurations.
- EXAMPLES FROM THE PLAY — include examples (e.g. quotes, context or events) that demonstrate understanding of the play and support the point you're making.
- DETAILED SUGGESTIONS — give specific details on how you would perform, design or direct a production that will help the examiner to visualise your ideas.
- EFFECT ON THE AUDIENCE — describe the desired effect of a production on the audience, as well as how this effect might be created using theatrical techniques.

... but extracts require a slightly different approach

If you're faced with an extract from your set play, there are other things to consider:

1) Read the question carefully. Then read through the extract and highlight any important words or phrases (including stage directions). You might also want to annotate the extract as you go along.
2) For a shorter question (see p.64), you'll only need to pick out one or two ideas from the extract. However, longer questions (see p.65) require you to group related ideas together in paragraphs.
3) Your answer should be coherent — not just a list of different possibilities for the extract. For example, if you start writing about a naturalistic approach, don't swap to a non-naturalistic one halfway through.

For all the questions, just remember — This. Is. DRAMA!

It's easy to lapse into analysing the performance text itself, but that's not what GCSE Drama is about. In the written exam, you need to put yourself in the shoes of a theatre maker — not an English student.

Set Text Question

Now that you've seen some questions, you must be desperate to read some answers... right? Either way, they're still worth looking at — they'll give you a better idea of what the examiner wants to see from you.

Shorter answers should be concise...

In the exam, you shouldn't spend too much time on short-answer questions that aren't worth many marks. Your answers will need to be snappy and straight to the point. Have a look at this example:

You are a costume designer for a production of *1984*.

Suggest a costume for Winston Smith and explain why your choices are appropriate.

'1984' is set in a dystopian version of 1980s Great Britain, in a society where everyone has their individuality taken away from them. Winston's costume should communicate this setting and time period to the audience, so I would suggest that he should wear a faded, white button-up shirt made from cotton, a dark brown, polyester tie and beige polyester trousers. This costume would make Winston blend in with the other characters and the scenery, as the plain colours would stop him from standing out.
Furthermore, Winston's tie would highlight his social status, because he is an office worker who belongs to the middle-class Outer Party.

This shows that you've considered the play's setting.

Give precise details (e.g. colour and material) to make your design ideas easier to visualise.

This demonstrates knowledge of the character and uses it to support the choice of costume.

... and full of evidence from the play

It's important to keep your answers concise, but you still need to back up your ideas with examples from the play and make sure you link everything back to the question. Here's another example answer:

You are going to play Gerald Croft in a production of *An Inspector Calls*.

Give two ways you would use vocal skills to communicate this character in this extract.

The extract referred to in this question is in Act 2 of the play.

In this extract, I would aim to portray Gerald as selfish and cruel for abandoning Daisy Renton and leaving her homeless.
I would use a casual tone and a regular pace when saying "I didn't feel about her as she felt about me" to reflect how unfeeling Gerald is towards Daisy. Later in the extract, Gerald tries to justify his behaviour to the Inspector. At this point, I would use a quieter voice, a concerned tone and a much slower pace to say "I never saw her again". This would make Gerald sound more serious, as though he wants to seem remorseful for treating Daisy so badly.

This states your intentions and shows a good understanding of the character.

The question asks for two uses of vocal skills, so you should give two examples.

This gives a clear description of the vocal skills used and links them back to the character.

Set Text Question

Longer answers should go into more detail

Questions that are worth more marks need longer, more detailed answers. However, everything you write should still be relevant to the question. Take a look at this extract from a longer answer:

> You are a set designer for a production of *Twelfth Night*.
>
> Explain how you would use set design to bring this extract to life for the audience.

The extract referred to in this question is in Act 1, Scene 1.

This extract is set in the palace of Duke Orsino. The palace is in Illyria, on the Adriatic coast, and Orsino is a wealthy character. I would use a naturalistic set design to communicate these important details to the audience in a way that stays true to real life.

Make it clear to the examiner what you want your set design to show.

To reflect the play's coastal setting, I would put a cyclorama in an upstage position and project a moving image of the sea onto it. This would make it look like the view from Orsino's palace. In front of the cyclorama, I would place a balcony made from an expensive-looking material like fake marble for Orsino to look out from. This would add to the lavish feel of the palace. The Adriatic coast has a pleasant climate, so I would put fake olive and pomegranate trees along the edges of the stage to reflect this setting.

Explain your ideas using accurate technical terms (e.g. cyclorama).

This demonstrates an awareness of the setting and applies it to the set design.

The set would consist of gleaming black and white tiles on the floor and white stone columns stage left and stage right to give the audience an impression of Duke Orsino's wealth. Orsino could lounge on a gold chaise longue at centre stage for the first line of the extract: "If music be the food of love, play on". The chaise longue's central position and gold material would highlight that he is the highest-status character.

Describe the effect of your set design on the audience.

Use quotes to tell the examiner which part of the extract you're talking about.

In this extract, the set would also need to accommodate the "Lords" and "Musicians" who are present, so I would leave a space near to the chaise longue for the Lords to stand, talk and drink goblets of wine. The musicians would stand downstage right and play lutes and recorders. These are traditional 17th-century instruments, so they would act as another reminder of the play's setting.

Use the correct terminology to explain exactly where things are on stage.

Try to link your ideas back to the play's context.

Exams are tricky — and that's the long and short of it...

Nobody said the written exam was going to be easy, but there's no need to panic. Everything will seem much less difficult once you've got to grips with the techniques for writing shorter and longer answers.

Live Theatre Evaluation

There's good news and bad news. The good news is that the set text question is done and dusted, but the bad news is that the live theatre evaluation is still to come — here's everything you need to know about it.

You'll need to analyse a live performance

1) The final section of the written exam concentrates on a live theatre performance of your choice. In this section, you'll still be expected to:

   Demonstrate knowledge and understanding of how drama is developed and performed **(AO3)**.

   ... but you'll also need to: *Analyse and evaluate your own work and the work of others* **(AO4)**.

2) In order to demonstrate these skills, you'll need to write about a theatre production that you've seen during the course. You'll usually be asked to focus on a specific aspect of this production.

> Analyse and evaluate how lighting and sound were used to enhance the impact of the production on the audience. You should consider:
>
> - types of lighting and sound
> - the effect of lighting and sound
> - your personal response to the production

Edexcel separate this question into two parts.

You might not always be given bullet points.

3) You're more likely to feel the full effect of a production if you're there in person. However, some exam boards let you write about streamed productions or digital recordings if you can't make it to a theatre.
4) You can write about any professional or amateur production — just not the work of your classmates.

Do your research before the performance...

1) If you want to get the most out of a live performance, you should prepare yourself for it in advance.
2) Start by familiarising yourself with the plot of the play you're going to watch — that way, you'll be able to focus on the way it's performed, designed and directed rather than the story itself.
3) After that, you might want to read some reviews of your chosen production. These are likely to pick out the most interesting features of the production, so they'll give you an idea of what to look out for.

... and make some notes as soon as it's finished

1) Making notes during the performance might seem like a good idea, but it'll distract you and make you miss key moments in the play. It's better to immerse yourself in the action and make notes afterwards.
2) As soon as the performance is finished, write down your observations in as much detail as possible. These notes should contain a personal response. In other words, you should include your opinion on which bits of the performance were effective, as well as which bits weren't.
3) If you're struggling to remember specific details about what you saw, try searching online for photos of the production to jog your memory.
4) Another useful way of revising is to put together a mood board — a collection of annotated images from key moments in the performance.

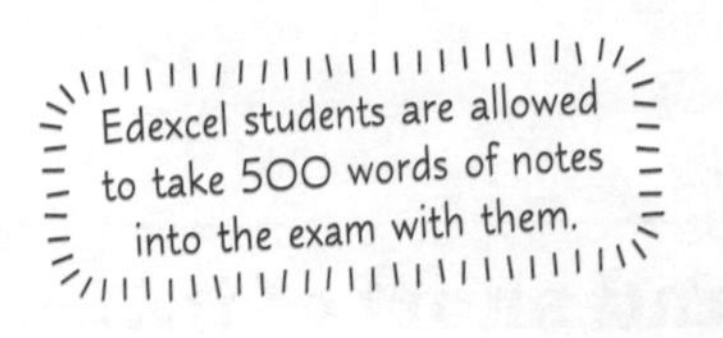

Live Theatre Evaluation

Your notes should cover all of the bases

There's no way of knowing which aspect of the live performance the written exam is going to ask about. That means you'll need to make comprehensive notes that cover all of the following points (and more)...

Performance

- You should try to look at the performers as individuals, but also as part of a cast — the way they work with each other is crucial.
- The performers are likely to combine vocal and physical skills throughout the performance, so you should write about both.
- It's important to think about what the performers were trying to achieve. This depends mainly on the style of the performance.

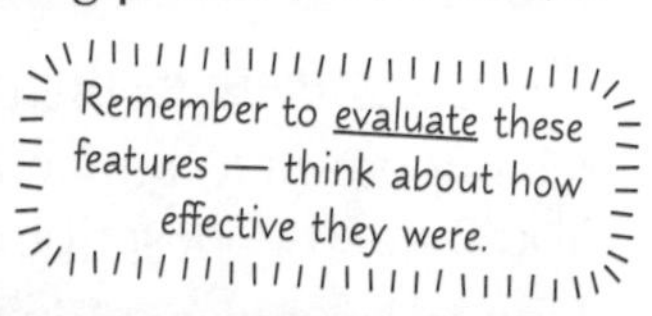

Think about the performers' use of space (e.g. proxemics) too — it's often a way of expressing the relationships between characters.

Costume Design

- Describe the costumes as precisely as possible — include details such as the size, material and colour.
- Costumes reveal more about the characters and context, but they can also have symbolic importance.
- Don't forget that small details like hair and make-up have an impact on the overall effect of a costume.

Staging and Set Design

- You should start with the type of stage used, as well as any larger constructions that were added to it.
- You'll need to consider how the performers interacted with the set, including the props and furniture.
- The set provides a sense of place, but it can support the action in other ways (e.g. to indicate style).

Don't forget to use technical language to describe each different design feature.

Keep an eye out for other aspects of design, like puppetry or animation.

Lighting and Sound

- As well as describing the lighting equipment used, you'll need to think about the colour, direction and intensity of the lights.
- You'll also need to include details like the rhythm and volume of any music and sound effects — not just how they were made.
- The lighting and sound contribute to the performance in several ways, but they're particularly important in creating atmosphere.

Develop an understanding of the director's vision

1) Every director has a vision — a clear idea of what they want their production to achieve. In your notes, you should try to establish whether the director of your chosen production was successful.
2) Many plays aim to get across a certain message or to make the audience feel a particular emotion. If you can figure out the purpose of the live performance that you saw, you'll understand it better.
3) You might find it useful to pick out some key moments from the performance. Many directors will make their intentions particularly obvious during the most important or dramatic parts of the story.

Proper planning prevents pitifully poor performance...

Going to the theatre is always an exciting experience, but the live theatre evaluation is a serious matter. If you want to achieve top marks, you'll need to put in the hard work before and after the performance.

Live Theatre Evaluation

Your notes might be the envy of all your classmates, but they're no use unless you can bring them together into a coherent answer on the day of the exam. Not to worry — these pages will show you how it's done.

Describe and analyse the play's features...

1) The live theatre evaluation tests three main skills — it requires you to describe, analyse and evaluate.
2) It's important to remember that the examiner probably hasn't seen the production you're writing about. You'll need to describe the performance clearly so that the examiner can visualise it for themselves.
3) However, you shouldn't narrate the plot — only describe something if it's relevant to the question.
4) Once you've described a feature of the performance, you'll need to analyse it. This involves identifying the techniques that were used and then explaining their intended effect on the audience.
5) You should describe and analyse each feature of the performance using appropriate technical vocabulary. If you don't, you'll struggle to get your point across to the examiner and it'll lose you marks.

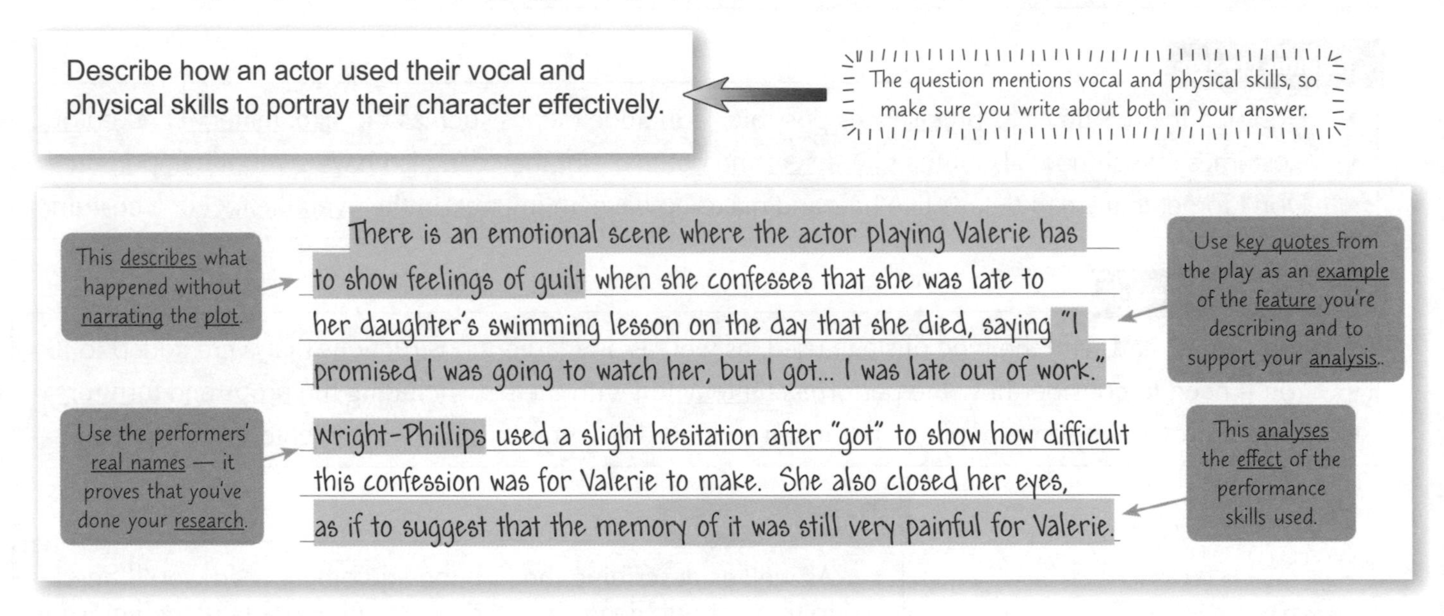

... and evaluate how successful they were

This example is just an extract from a full answer.

1) You should evaluate every feature that you describe and analyse. This means asking yourself whether the director, performer or designer achieved what they set out to achieve, before sharing your opinion.
2) It's fine to criticise the production, but you'll need to back up your point of view with good examples. Ideally, you would make constructive suggestions for how it might have been performed differently.

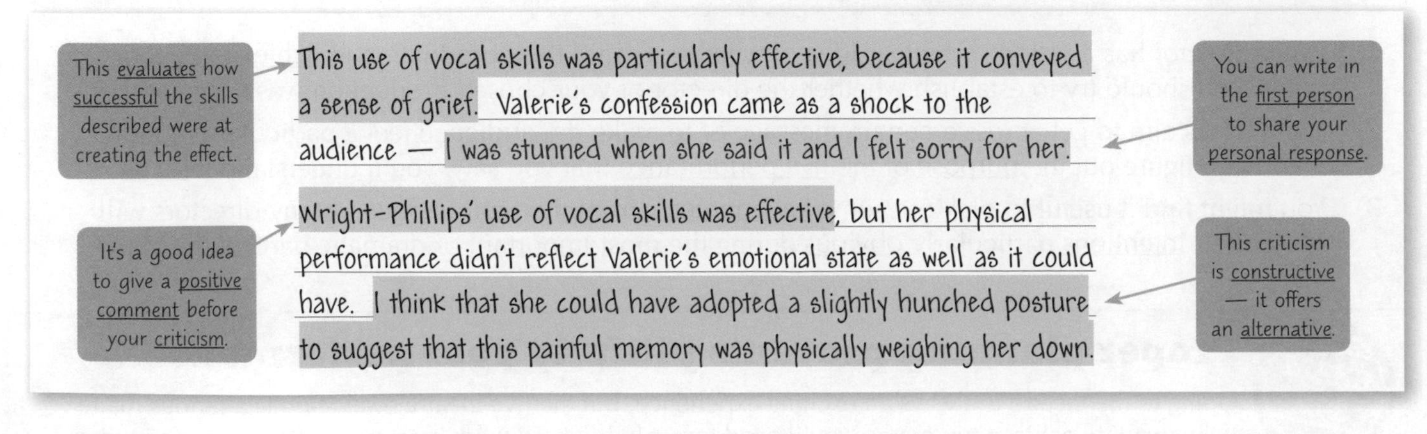

Live Theatre Evaluation

The evaluation is a long-answer question

The live theatre evaluation is usually worth quite a lot of marks, so you should treat it like one of the longer set-text questions (see p.65). In other words, you should group any related points into paragraphs and write in as much detail as possible. The answer below is a good example of how you might get started.

Analyse and evaluate how sound effects and music were used to enhance the impact of the production.

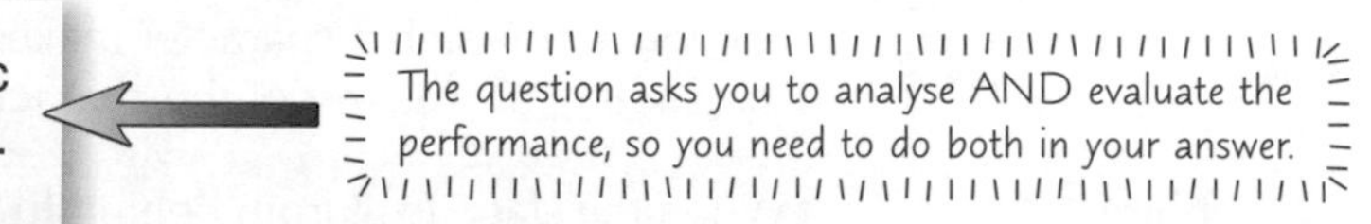

Always start by telling the examiner what you saw and when you saw it.

I saw a production of 'Amadeus' at the Olivier Theatre on Thursday 15th February. It was a stage dramatisation of the lives of Wolfgang Amadeus Mozart and Antonio Salieri, directed by Michael Longhurst. As a play about the bitter rivalry between two composers, it featured several scenes in which sound effects and music were used to enhance the impact of the production on the audience.

Using the wording of the question will help keep your answer focused.

All of the music was produced on stage by a live orchestra that contained a wide range of stringed, woodwind and brass instruments. This orchestra was integrated into the action — the musicians stood alongside the actors on stage, although they didn't wear costumes.

Tell the examiner how the sound effects and music were produced.

This makes it clear exactly what part of the play you're talking about.

A particularly significant use of music occurred when Salieri read one of Mozart's compositions for the first time. The orchestra began to play every time Salieri opened the book containing Mozart's music. This gave the audience the impression that he was playing the music over and over again in his head. Also, the music started quietly and slowly with a small number of stringed instruments, before building in volume and pace as the scene went on. This suggested that Salieri was becoming increasingly frustrated while he read through Mozart's work.

This considers the impact of the music on the audience.

Use accurate terminology to provide the examiner with precise details.

I thought that this use of music was particularly effective, because it gave me a clear insight into Salieri's mind that dialogue alone would have struggled to achieve. The whole scene made me feel very tense, because it conveyed Salieri's jealousy of Mozart's talent and hinted at his determination to bring about Mozart's downfall — the starting and stopping of the orchestral music helped to create this tense atmosphere.

This evaluates the success of the feature identified.

This shares a personal response to the performance.

This is just an extract. The answer would go on to consider the use of sound effects as well.

EXAM TIP

Repeat after me — describe, analyse, evaluate...

Describe, analyse, evaluate. Describe, analyse, evaluate. You'll be muttering these words to yourself in your sleep before you know it, but that's not such a bad thing — they're the key to exam success.

Glossary

ad-libbing	When an actor delivers all or part of a performance without preparation.
alienation effect	When theatre makers use techniques (such as minimal scenery or undeveloped characters) to remind the audience that what they are watching isn't real.
antagonist	A character who causes trouble for the protagonist.
aside	A comment which a character makes to another character or the audience. The rest of the characters on stage can't hear them.
backlighting	When the stage is lit from behind to produce silhouettes of the actors.
backstory	The events that have happened to a character before the action of the play.
barndoor	A metal flap that can be attached to a stage lantern and used to shape its light beam.
Berkoff, Steven	A British theatre maker who uses actors' bodies to convey a story rather than sets.
black box studio	A small theatre with a black interior. The seating can be rearranged to suit the performance.
blackout	When the stage lights are turned off between scenes or at the end of a performance.
blocking	The process of positioning the actors on stage and planning their movements to maintain good sightlines for the audience.
body language	The way movements, posture and gestures can show how someone feels without speaking.
box set	A naturalistic set made up of a complete room with one side open to the audience.
Brecht, Bertolt	A German theatre maker who played a major role in the development of epic theatre.
catharsis	The sense of release felt by an audience when a play makes them feel strong emotions.
character arc	The way a character changes over the course of a story.
characterisation	The way an actor interprets and performs their character.
choreography	A rehearsed sequence of steps or movements.
chorus	A group of third-person narrators who provide extra information about the plot and comment on the action or characters. Originally a feature of Ancient Greek theatre.
cliffhanger	When a conflict isn't fully resolved, leaving the audience wondering what happens next.
climax	The turning point in a play, where tension is at its highest. When the tension is resolved again straight away, this can create an anticlimax.
comedy	A genre of drama which features humour and a happy ending.
commedia dell'arte	A type of comedy popular in 16th to 18th-century Italy that makes use of stock characters.
composite set	A set which shows multiple locations on stage at the same time.
cross-cutting	When two or more scenes which take place at different times or in different places are performed on stage at the same time.
cue	A signal that tells the actors or technicians when a certain action needs to take place.
cyclical structure	A plot structure which starts and finishes at the same point in the narrative.
cyclorama	A curved screen at the back of the stage which can have scenery projected onto it.

Glossary

dialogue	The general term for any lines spoken between characters.
diction	The quality (or clarity) of a performer's vocal expression.
documentary theatre	A genre which tells real-life stories using factual sources (e.g. newspapers) as inspiration.
downlighting	When the stage is lit from above to highlight certain characters or cast shadows.
dramatic irony	When the audience knows something that the characters don't.
duologue	A scene or section of dialogue which only involves two actors.
emotional arc	How the protagonist's emotions and state of mind change throughout the play.
epic theatre	A style of theatre made famous by Bertolt Brecht. It tries to distance the audience from the action of the play so that they can concentrate on the overall message.
epilogue	A closing scene or speech that comes after the main action of the play.
exposition	The part of a plot which introduces the main characters and hints at the play's later conflict.
falling action	The part of a plot which settles the conflict (it might contain one last moment of suspense).
farce	A type of comedy which features improbable situations and physical humour.
flashback / flashforward	A scene which shows events from before or after the main action of the play. It can give extra information about the plot or help to develop characters.
flat	A wooden frame with canvas stretched over it which is painted and used as scenery.
floodlight	A type of stage lantern which casts a broad wash of light onto the stage.
flying rig	A piece of equipment that the actors can be suspended from to create the illusion of flight.
foil	A secondary character who contrasts with the protagonist.
form	The type of written drama (e.g. play, opera, musical, pantomime). These often have set theatrical conventions, but vary in genre and style.
forum theatre	A style of theatre where a short play showing a form of injustice is performed twice. The audience are encouraged to intervene in the second performance to change its outcome.
fourth wall	The imaginary barrier that separates the audience from the world of the play on stage.
freeze frame	When the performers suddenly stop the action at a key moment.
fresnel spotlight	A type of stage lantern which casts a beam with a softly defined edge.
gel	A piece of coloured, heat-resistant, plastic film used to change the colour of a lantern's beam.
genre	The type of story a play is telling (e.g. comedy, tragedy).
gesture	A movement made by part of the body (e.g. arms, head) to convey a character's emotions.
gobo	A thin, metal disc with shapes cut into it which can be slotted into a lantern to project patterns or images onto the stage or a backdrop.
hot-seating	A rehearsal technique where an actor stays in character and answers questions from the rest of the group. The aim is to develop a better understanding of the character.

Glossary

immersive theatre	A style of theatre which removes the barrier between the actors and the audience by actively involving the audience in the performance.
improvisation	When drama is made up on the spot by performers without using any prepared material.
incidental music	Any music which accompanies a performance and is used to create mood or tension.
intonation	The rise and fall of a performer's voice to create a natural pattern of speech.
invisible theatre	A style of theatre developed by Brazilian theatre maker Augusto Boal where a public performance is disguised as a real-life situation in order to encourage onlookers to intervene.
lighting rig	A structure above the stage and wings which holds the stage lanterns.
linear structure	A plot structure where the events on stage happen in chronological order.
mannerism	A repeated physical or vocal habit that contributes to characterisation.
marking the moment	A technique that draws the audience's attention to an important moment (e.g. slow motion).
mask	A full or partial covering for the face (or a performance in which the actors wear these).
melodrama	A genre of theatre that features unbelievable plots, extreme emotions and exaggerated acting. The effect is often heightened using incidental music.
method acting	A technique where an actor fully immerses themselves in their role.
mime	The use of movements, gestures and facial expressions to communicate an idea without words.
minimalist theatre	A genre of theatre which uses a basic set and very few props or simple costumes.
minor character	A character who isn't important to the plot but adds depth to the world of the play.
mixing desk	A piece of equipment that can be used to control the volume of different sounds.
monologue	A speech made by one character, either to another character or the audience.
mood	The atmosphere at a particular moment that creates a feeling or emotion for the audience.
musical theatre	A style of theatre that uses song and dance to develop the plot and entertain the audience.
narrator	A character who comments on the action and the plot to the audience. The narrator can be first-person (involved in the action) or third-person (set apart from the action).
naturalism	A style of theatre which tries to recreate real life on stage as closely as possible.
non-linear structure	When the events of a plot aren't shown in chronological order.
parcan	A stage lantern with an adjustable beam which can produce bright, coloured washes.
parody	A form of comedy which makes fun of an existing dramatic work or style by imitating it.
phrasing	The way a character's dialogue is broken up into sections when spoken by an actor.
physical theatre	A non-naturalistic style of theatre which uses physical movements to tell stories.
plot	The series of events that takes place in a play.
posture	The position a character holds themselves in when sitting or standing.

Glossary

profile spotlight	A type of stage lantern that produces a sharply defined beam. These lanterns are used to focus on a particular character or part of the stage.
prologue	An opening scene or speech that comes before the main action of the play.
promenade theatre	A style of theatre that requires the audience to follow the actors between different performance spaces over the course of the play. This usually takes place outdoors.
prompt book	An annotated copy of the script that contains every detail about the performance, including technical cues.
prop	An item on stage that the characters can interact with. If a prop is specific to one character, it's called a personal prop.
proscenium arch stage	A box-shaped stage which is set back from the audience so that only the front end is open to them, framed by the proscenium arch itself.
protagonist	The main character in a story.
proxemics	The use of the physical space between the actors on stage to create meaning.
pyrotechnics	A theatrical firework display which is used to create dramatic effects on stage.
realism	A heightened form of naturalism that aims to be exactly like real life.
resolution	The section of a plot where any loose ends left over from the falling action are tied up.
revolving stage	A stage or part of a stage which can spin around.
rising action	The section of a plot which develops the conflict and builds tension.
role on the wall	A rehearsal technique that involves writing thoughts, opinions and personality traits inside a character's outline to aid characterisation.
rostrum (plural rostra)	A raised platform which is used to introduce different levels to the stage.
satire	A type of comedy which mocks something serious by making it seem ridiculous.
set model	A small, scale model of the set which helps to visualise the set designer's ideas.
shadow theatre	A piece of theatre created using a bright backlight which casts shadows on a partially see-through screen between the performers and audience.
silhouette	A dark outline of the performers or scenery which is created using a backlight.
site-specific theatre	A style of staging which temporarily transforms somewhere that isn't a theatre into a performance space. This space often resembles the play's setting in some way.
slapstick	A type of comedy that features exaggerated movements and physical humour.
soliloquy	When a character speaks their mind to the audience, but can't be heard by anyone on stage.
soundscape	A collection of individual sounds that are layered up to create a strong sense of place.
split stage	When the stage is split into different areas representing different places or times.
stage directions	Any instructions written in a script by the playwright to explain how a play should be performed.
stage furniture	Any moveable object on stage which isn't a costume, a prop or a part of the scenery.

Glossary

stagehand	A theatre maker who works backstage and helps to set up and change the scenery and props.
Stanislavski, Konstantin	A Russian theatre maker who had a major role in the development of naturalistic theatre.
stimulus (plural stimuli)	A starting point for your devised piece that you should use to inspire your performance.
stock character	A character who is based on a common stereotype.
stress	In vocal performance, the emphasis a performer places on certain words and phrases.
strobe	A type of stage lantern which rapidly flashes on and off.
structure	The shape of a play's narrative, including the order in which it's shown to the audience.
style	The way in which a director chooses to interpret a performance text on stage.
subplot	A storyline which is less important than the main plot.
subtext	The underlying or hidden meaning behind a character's speech and actions.
supporting character	A character who is important to the plot but isn't the audience's main focus.
suspension of disbelief	The willingness of the audience to temporarily accept that what they're watching is real.
symbolism	The use of props, gestures, setting, lighting etc to represent other things and create meaning.
tableau	A moment in a performance when the action stops and the characters freeze in position.
theatre in the round	A style of staging which seats the audience on all sides of a central stage.
theatre maker	The name given to anyone who is involved in staging a performance.
Theatre of Cruelty	A style of theatre which aims to create extreme emotions in the audience by using shock tactics such as bright lights, loud sounds and striking physical movements.
Theatre of the Oppressed	A collection of techniques which aim to change the audience's attitudes by involving them in a performance (e.g. invisible theatre, forum theatre).
thought tracking	When a character tells the audience their thoughts during a pause in the action.
thrust stage	A stage which extends out into the audience, so that they're seated on three sides.
tragedy	A genre of play which features a serious plot and an unhappy ending.
tragic hero	The protagonist of a tragedy, whose flaws lead to their downfall (or death).
tragicomedy	A genre which combines elements of comedy and tragedy in the same story.
traverse stage	A long, narrow stage which runs between the audience, who face the stage on both sides.
truck	A structure on wheels which can be painted on both sides and used as scenery.
understudy	Someone who learns a performer's role so they can replace them if necessary.
uplighting	When the stage is lit from below to create an unusual or unsettling effect.
verbatim theatre	A variation on documentary theatre that involves repeating factual sources word for word.
wings	The space to the side of a stage which is used for storage and as a waiting area for the actors.

Index

Index